# TRAVELING IN BARDO

# TRAVELING IN BARDO

## THE ART OF LIVING IN AN IMPERMANENT WORLD

# ANN TASHI SLATER

balance

New York  Boston

Copyright © 2025 by Ann Tashi Davis Slater

Cover Design by Grace Han
Cover Images © Hyder Jung Hearsey via British Library Archive/Bridgeman Images; CSA Images/Getty
Cover copyright © 2025 by Hachette Book Group, Inc.

Hachette Book Group supports the right to free expression and the value of copyright. The purpose of copyright is to encourage writers and artists to produce the creative works that enrich our culture.

The scanning, uploading, and distribution of this book without permission is a theft of the author's intellectual property. If you would like permission to use material from the book (other than for review purposes), please contact Permissions@hbgusa.com. Thank you for your support of the author's rights.

Any third-party content used in this book is the property of the respective owners and the use of such material does not imply the owners' endorsement or authorization of this book.

Balance
Hachette Book Group
1290 Avenue of the Americas
New York, NY 10104
GCP-Balance.com
@GCPBalance

First Edition: September 2025

Balance is an imprint of Grand Central Publishing. The Balance name and logo are registered trademarks of Hachette Book Group, Inc.

The publisher is not responsible for websites (or their content) that are not owned by the publisher.

The Hachette Speakers Bureau provides a wide range of authors for speaking events. To find out more, visit hachettespeakersbureau.com or email HachetteSpeakers@hbgusa.com.

Balance books may be purchased in bulk for business, educational, or promotional use. For information, please contact your local bookseller or email the Hachette Book Group Special Markets Department at Special.Markets@hbgusa.com.

Print book interior design by Bart Dawson

Library of Congress Cataloging-in-Publication Data

Name: Slater, Ann Tashi author
Title: Traveling in bardo: the art of living in an impermanent world / Ann Tashi Slater.
Description: First edition. | New York: Balance, 2025. | Includes bibliographical references.
Identifiers: LCCN 2025010847 | ISBN 9780306835216 hardcover | ISBN 9780306835223 trade paperback | ISBN 9780306835230 ebook
Subjects: LCSH: Self-actualization (Psychology)—Religious Aspects—Buddhism | Impermanence (Buddhism)
Classification: LCC BF637.S4 S5845 2025 | DDC 294.3/444—dc23/eng/20250603
LC record available at https://lccn.loc.gov/2025010847

ISBNs: 978-0-306-83521-6 (hardcover); 978-0-306-83523-0 (ebook)

Printed in the United States of America

LSC-C

Printing 1, 2025

*For David*

*Photograph courtesy of Ann Tashi Slater*

# CONTENTS

*Foreword by Dani Shapiro* • xiii
*Prologue* • xix

**1.**
My Grandmother's Funeral • 1
*A Window into Life*

**2.**
Tibet to India to California • 21

**3.**
Coming to Realize You Are Dead • 45

**4.**
Play, Engage, Stop and Pay Attention • 75

**5.**
Taking Bardo by the Forelock • 107

**6.**
We Might Die Tonight • 145

**7.**
Hail-Storms and Whirlwinds of Icy Blasts • 177
*A Bardo Journey*

**8.**
We Are the Artists of Our Lives • 211

*Epilogue* • 241

*Acknowledgments* • 247
*Sources and Works Consulted* • 251

# TRAVELING
IN BARDO

# FOREWORD
## By Dani Shapiro

A friend of mine sent a note recently, letting me know about the declining health of a mutual friend of ours in Los Angeles. Days later, she wrote to tell me that he had died. He was ninety. There was so much shock in her response to losing this person who had lived a long, full life. Reading her email, I realized that over the years, my view of impermanence—of life and death—has changed dramatically.

My first experience with profound loss was the death of my father in a car accident. I was twenty-three and he was in his early sixties. He left behind unfinished business, including a life insurance policy he hadn't gotten around to signing. That kind of thing, together with the sudden and violent way I lost him, brought home to me the ephemerality of life. And what exactly is "finished business," anyway?

I found myself thinking a great deal about how my father had lived. He walked around with a lot of alarm, a sense of imminent danger, of impending doom, that didn't allow him to truly be in the present. He lived in a place of fear, and then his fears came true. I didn't want to live like that. I wanted to be able to hold the knowledge that we cannot predict or prevent danger, that we have no idea on any given day what's around the corner. I also wanted for that knowledge not to crush me.

But in my twenties and into my early thirties, I found myself living in a state much like my father's; I was afraid. I fell in love and got married and became a mother. All good things. But my son had a rare disease as a baby and one of my first thoughts was that I'd let my guard down. As if *my guard* would have made any difference! I felt like I hadn't girded myself against my son's illness, in the same way I hadn't girded myself against my dad's death, which had come at me like a fist through a veil.

My son miraculously recovered, and now he's a thriving and healthy twenty-five-year-old man. But the knowledge that it could have been otherwise has stayed with me ever since. That's where my tender opening began, this feeling of *it could have been otherwise* and, at some point, *will* be otherwise, for all of us.

*Otherwise* came for my mother when she was eighty and died of lung cancer. As the end approached, she told me, "I was just getting my life together." I found it so heartbreaking that she felt that way. After her death, I was cleaning out her apartment and discovered that her closets were filled with blank notebooks. She would go out and buy notebooks, with all these intentions about what she was going to write in them. What would she have done differently if she'd reckoned with the reality that her time could be up at any moment? She died profoundly unhappy, and that also had a huge impact on me and my sense of time—how little we have, how uncertain we are about how to spend it, cherish it, and even relinquish it.

A little over a decade after I lost my mother, I learned from a recreational DNA test that my beloved dad had not been my biological father. Impermanence. Loss. Gain. *No idea on any given day what's around the corner.* But in a way, I'd always known this about my dad. I'd spent years writing about families and the corrosive power of secrets, digging for something that I somehow knew but kept secret from myself. We keep secrets from ourselves because we feel like if we don't, we're not going to be able to walk down the street and go to the grocery store and go to the movies and love our people. But as shocking and destabilizing as it was to find out about my father, it also liberated me.

I wrote about this discovery and experience in my own book, *Inheritance*. (Sounds a whole lot like *Impermanence*, I realize now.) The book reached a lot of readers, and its publication marked a wonderful moment in my career. But during this same time—because time is an impartial player—my husband was diagnosed with a serious cancer.

Thus began the greatest lesson I've learned so far in holding cognitive dissonance: the presence of both death and vibrant aliveness. The worst moment in my life, the terror that I was going to lose my husband, existed *together* with the thrilling thing that was happening with my tenth book, that had never happened to me before and likely would never happen again. I took care of my husband, and I also went out in the world to promote my memoir. I tried to find a balance, not in the usual way we talk about balance—it's a myth that we can have everything balanced—but in the sense that wherever I was, I was there fully.

My husband was cured after a long and arduous ordeal, and that was another miracle.

I recently learned that I had a rare and small cancer in my eye. It was caught early, so I'm pretty confident that this is not going to be the thing that gets me. Still, the way I walk through the world is changing as I gradually lose vision in my right eye. This, a certain, definitive loss. So where is the gain? And what's around the corner? Presented with this paradigm yet again, I realize my job as a human is to live in that place of, "What am I learning? How can I make meaning of this? How can I grow from this and share it?"

If I thought of the difficult things that have happened to me as fate, I would despair, but I experience them as karma, as *action*, in the sense that as I've moved through them, I've learned and changed.

I feel like I'm living well. I'm finding meaning and happiness. In the miracles *and* the fear. I have been thrust into an acute awareness of the preciousness of life. It is precarious, too—this big, rich human experience. It is scary. It is beautiful. Fleeting and fulfilling and so very full. I feel a deep consciousness of mortality, of aging, of what it is to be in a human body. Most of all, I feel at peace. It's a profound pleasure to think, "I'm going to love this day, this moment."

I live in New England, and there's snow on the fields outside right now. As the light comes streaming in, I quietly observe and appreciate. I'm experiencing an evolving communion with nature, with the world, with my loved ones, and myself. It will all be gone soon, and yet. And yet. This *moment*. The deeper I go inside of it, the more I am free to roam in bardo and absorb the wisdom that Ann Tashi Slater shares with us in this gorgeous book.

Exploring joy and grief, love and loss, through the lens of *The Tibetan Book of the Dead*, our literary and cultural landscape, her Tibetan family history, and her own experiences of bardo, Slater brings us to a profound understanding of the things that matter most to us. How can we become more accepting of change? How can we live with empathy, attention, and kindness amid the beauty and sorrow of this ephemeral world? Knowing we may or may not have tomorrow, how can we embrace life fully now? These are the questions that Slater asks and so beautifully answers in *Traveling in Bardo*, guiding us on our journey in the bardo from birth to death and showing us how to live in this impermanent world.

# PROLOGUE

Stars glitter over twenty-eight-thousand-foot Mount Kanchenjunga and a coal fire burns in the grate as my grandmother and I chat in her cozy living room decorated with Tibetan carpets, *thangka* scroll paintings of the Buddha's life, and old family photographs. The odor of incense wafts from the prayer room down the hall, and outside, my grandmother's Lhasa Apsos bark at people real and imagined passing in the lane. The train whistles—one long, two short—as it pulls into Darjeeling Station down near the marketplace.

I've just graduated from college and flown around the world from San Francisco to keep my recently widowed grandmother company. Not wanting to waste a minute of our time together, she invites family friends for meals, takes me for joyrides in her olive-green Ambassador, and regales me with stories of Tibet, turn-of-the-century Darjeeling, my mother's girlhood, and our ancestors.

Over the years, I'll return often to continue our conversations. Many of my grandmother's stories are about her father, and one in particular will plant the seed for this book: Just after World War I, my great-grandfather helped bring *The Tibetan Book of the Dead* to the West, the first English translation of the eighth-century *Bardo Thödol*. In Tibetan Buddhism, *bardo* refers to a between-state, or period of transition. The *Bardo Thödol* was written to help the dead navigate the bardo between death and rebirth, and to guide us, the living, on our journey through the bardo between birth and death.

During over forty years of writing and speaking about my family history and Buddhism, I've come to see how Tibetan bardo wisdom on the fleeting nature of existence can transform the way we live. By showing us how to become more accepting of the uncertainty, transitions, and endings we all must face sooner or later, the bardo teachings free us to live more fully, embracing life in all its sorrow and joy.

I dreamed once that I was being blessed by a Tibetan lama. He said, "You can tell the story coming down through the generations." I took this to mean my personal story and the story of my family, but as I've learned about *The Tibetan Book of the Dead* and bardo, I've come to see that it's also our collective story: what it means to live well, for us as individuals and as part of a family, a community, and a global society.

*Traveling in Bardo: The Art of Living in an Impermanent World* is not intended as an exhaustive account or

## PROLOGUE

explanation of *The Tibetan Book of the Dead*, but rather as a consideration of how the bardo teachings can help us live happier lives. I'll draw on my girlhood in America and many years in Tokyo, as well as time spent in Darjeeling and my decades of research on Buddhism, to explore how the words of this ancient manual can benefit us today. My book begins with my grandmother's traditional funeral, one of the last that will ever be held, followed by a look at the origins of *The Tibetan Book of the Dead*, my family connection to it, and the enduring fascination with bardo. Together, we'll then explore bardo principles like acceptance, interdependence, and impermanence in relation to friendship and marriage, children and parents, and work and creativity.

Life brings change, whether it's a new stage, such as becoming a parent or moving to another city, or the loss of someone we love, growing old, or our own death. This book is about how we can find deeper meaning and fresh direction in a world where transitions are not only inevitable but can come at any moment. As my grandmother liked to say, "Happiness is there for everyone, if only we will realize it." I hope my book will open new perspectives for you on how to find happiness in our impermanent world.

# TRAVELING IN BARDO

# 1.

# MY GRANDMOTHER'S FUNERAL

*A Window into Life*

O nobly-born…, the time hath now come for thee to seek the Path in reality.

—*The Tibetan Book of the Dead*

On a winter afternoon in 2004, I landed at a tiny airport north of Calcutta and began the sad journey into the Himalayas for my grandmother's funeral. The taxi driver sped up the winding road that I'd first traveled over forty years earlier on my mother's lap, when I was a small girl and visiting Darjeeling with my parents. Now I gazed out at the familiar tea gardens and villages, the dense forests of bamboo and palms and wild orchids. Soon the car was enveloped in swirling mist, all coming and going as in dreamtime: a wizened man standing outside a cottage holding a sickle, monkeys scampering by the roadside, prayer flags fluttering over a gorge, four lamas walking single file down a dirt path, their robes vermilion in the gloom.

I reached Darjeeling at twilight, as the snowy peaks of Mount Kanchenjunga were vanishing into the blue like great ships setting sail. Along the road, shoppers thronged the market stalls, buying live chickens, vegetables, spices, snacks, and sundries. A barefoot boy hawked bracelets, crying out in a high, singsong voice. As we passed the railway station and made the hairpin turn into my grandmother's lane, I felt afraid, because for the first time, my grandmother wouldn't be waiting for me at the door to her little house. When I had come to see her over the years, I'd always arrived late in the day, and she was ready with cucumber sandwiches and freshly brewed Darjeeling tea.

But now, instead, there would be tea for the people streaming in to pay their respects.

I started up the polished wooden stairs to the second floor, the same stairs my mother used to take two at a time after school, hungry for the momo dumplings and fried flour jalebis my grandmother would put out in the dining room; the stairs that my mother carried me up when I was a little girl; that I climbed when I lived with my grandmother after college and that my own children bounded up when we came for visits. The same stairs my grandmother's body would be brought down in a few days, when the death ceremonies were finished and she left her house for the very last time.

My mother had already arrived from her home in California and was on the landing greeting condolence callers.

"She was the grand old lady of Darjeeling," people were saying. "A legend."

"No one will replace her."

"It's the end of an era."

I walked with my mother along the hall to the altar room, where the prayers for my grandmother were underway. In the glow of butter lamps burning on the old altar carved with the Tibetan lucky symbols, five red-robed lamas sat next to my grandmother's body, which lay on cushions under a mound of white *khada* blessing scarves. In low, incantatory voices, the lamas were reading from *The Tibetan Book of the Dead*, encouraging my grandmother to move forward without fear in the *bardo* between death and rebirth.

"Would you like to see your grandmother?" my mother asked in a matter-of-fact voice. Raised as a Buddhist and trained as a physician, she had a pragmatic attitude toward death. She used to tell me and my siblings hair-raising stories about the cadavers she dissected in medical school, or, if she'd been working that day in the ER, about someone impaled on a piece of farm equipment or paralyzed in a motorcycle crash. But not only was I nervous about being so close to a dead body, it also seemed that if I didn't look, I wouldn't have to acknowledge that my grandmother was gone. When my mother called me at my home in Tokyo to say that her mother had died, I was stunned, though I shouldn't have been. Born in 1905, my grandmother was almost a hundred years old—How long did I think she was going to live? Still, it happened so suddenly. Returning from a trip to see friends in the south of India, she felt her body start to wind down, and soon her kidneys began to fail.

"I'm not sure I can look at her body," I told my mother, but she was already pulling back the khada scarves. My grandmother's thin hair lay in wisps around her forehead and her eye sockets were dark purple. I touched her sunken cheeks; her skin felt soft and cold. She was wearing only a thin flannel nightgown—Did she need a blanket?

I gazed for long moments, certain I'd detect a trace of her, a sign that even a small part of her was still alive. But a terrible sorrow took hold of me as I realized I was only looking at a body, a vessel that had once held my grandmother.

As if hearing my thoughts, my mother told me that when my grandmother died at 1:16 that morning, the lamas were summoned to conduct *phowa*, a ceremony to transfer the consciousness from the body. It was possible that my grandmother could reach enlightenment through phowa, in which case she would not travel through bardo, but, just to be safe, the prayers from *The Tibetan Book of the Dead* were being read to help her navigate the after-death journey.

With aunts, uncles, cousins, and other relations, my mother and I listened to the prayers. In the doorway at the back of the altar room that led to the kitchen, the household staff stood watching, bringing hot water for the lamas to drink during breaks. "Instead of tea," one of the cousins said, "because the lamas are getting health-conscious." The sound of hammering came from outside in the driveway, where some men were building a coffin. In the study next to the altar room, the *tsipa* astrologer lama was casting the death horoscope by consulting the texts he'd laid out on the teak desk where my grandmother used to write in her diary and my grandfather had composed letters to my mother on his Hermes Baby typewriter after she left for America.

The horoscope indicated that the cremation should take place in two days: Friday, December 3, at 9 a.m. "How about Saturday or Sunday?" my mother asked, hoping to give relatives who lived far away time to arrive. The tsipa shook his head. Saturday was never an auspicious day for a funeral, and if it was held on Sunday, nine members of the family would die.

Around seven o'clock that evening, my mother and I left for the Windamere, my grandparents' Raj-era hotel. The car bumped past the three-story house in the bazaar, where at the turn of the century my grandmother had read Jane Austen by candlelight; up past the colonial-style Planters Club, established for local tea planters in the 1800s; past blue-domed Government House, once the British governor of Bengal's summer residence; and then to the stone and stucco buildings of the Windamere at the top of town, overlooking Chowrasta, the main square. Farther up, on Observatory Hill, tall cryptomeria trees were silhouetted in the darkening evening, and down in the valleys, lights winked on like reflections of the planets and stars appearing in the sky.

We ate fish curry, okra masala, and English trifle in the hotel's candlelit dining room, 1920s London jazz playing low and the tables filled with guests from India and around the world. After dinner, my mother adjourned to the bar for a nightcap with her cousins and I went to bed. As I lay under the wool blankets, listening to dogs bark back and forth in the valleys, I imagined my grandmother setting off in bardo in her black poodle bouclé coat, her headscarf knotted under her chin. She had her usual determined, optimistic expression, and her short, solid figure rocked side to side in the gait I knew well. I saw her going forth in the same fearless way that in 1924, when she was nineteen, she left Darjeeling for Tibet on her pony Graylock ("He ambled so nicely on the precipices") to join her father in Lhasa, an expedition of hundreds of miles over snowy passes as high as fifteen thousand feet.

Crossing the Tibetan Plateau, my grandmother came upon great caravans miles long, and the muleteers offered her slices of raw yak meat. She encountered French explorer and Buddhist Alexandra David-Néel, the first Western woman to reach Lhasa, traveling down to India. Now, in bardo, perhaps my grandmother was breaking her journey at a dak bungalow, just as she did on the way to Lhasa. (Dak bungalows, rest houses built by the British, were found in the most far-flung places—surely one existed in the afterworld.) If only I could go to wherever she was on her bardo journey and bring her back. But even if it were possible to discover her whereabouts, it wouldn't matter, because she'd know that, just as she'd always told me when people died, the time had come to give up her old body and think about finding a new one.

~

In the morning, my mother and I returned to my grandmother's house, where the lamas were continuing with the prayers. Friends and relatives crowded into the altar room, arriving from Kalimpong, Sikkim, and Calcutta. They offered incense and khada scarves, talked with my mother, and explained things to me, the American granddaughter.

"These lamas are doing the prayers nicely, but the lamas who skip pages end up crushed in one of the hells by a very heavy prayer book big as Kanchenjunga."

"Your grandmother was born in the year of the serpent, so now her body looks to her like a dead serpent."

"Your grandmother can easily hear, even better than when she was alive."

The lamas' chanting rose and fell steadily, punctuated by bursts of cymbals and bells, horns and drums. I liked the idea that my grandmother could hear the prayers that she would have heard often during her long life. Maybe the first time was in Darjeeling in 1911, when she was six and her mother collapsed and died while bowing to a high lama who had come to the house to conduct a ceremony. The next time might have been when one of her older brothers was struck down by double pneumonia, and then when another brother succumbed to meningitis. She would have heard the bardo prayers in the altar rooms of old Tibetan homes in the 1920s, when she was in Lhasa. She heard the same prayers when her father died in 1936, and perhaps years later at funerals for friends who were killed after the Chinese took over Tibet in the 1950s, "dragged round and round," she told me, "and put in the black cellar as punishment, whipped to death." She heard the prayers when my grandfather died in 1980 and she sat next to his body just as we were now sitting next to hers.

In the flickering light of the butter lamps, I gazed at the room I knew so well. Next to the altar hung the black-and-white photos of deceased relatives: my grandfather, an aunt, an uncle. On the far wall was a *thangka* scroll painting of the Tibetan Buddhist master and yogi Milarepa; clad in white cotton, he held a hand to his ear, symbolizing the insight we can gain through listening. A string of letters spelling out "HA PY NEW YEAR" (the first P had been missing for as long as I could remember) was tied to the bottom, with a paper cutout of Donald Duck swinging from the middle.

In this room, generations of our family had prayed. It was here that my grandmother had taught my mother the prayers she learned from her father. This was where my grandmother brought me and my children at the end of our visits from Tokyo, touched our foreheads to the altar, and in a high, sweet voice said, "Happy landings!"

On the altar, offerings to the buddhas and bodhisattvas of all directions had been arranged: silver cups filled with rice and dried flowers, *torma* flour-and-butter sculptures, and *chang* rice beer, which the deities were said to be especially fond of. Next to these stood my grandmother's prayer wheel and prayer book. In the glass cabinet above were statues of Gautama, the Historical Buddha; Maitreya, the Future Buddha; and Guru Rinpoche, the Indian sage who, centuries ago, helped to bring Buddhism to Tibet and, according to legend, composed *The Tibetan Book of the Dead*.

The direct translation of the book's Tibetan title, *Bardo Thödol*, is "Liberation in the Intermediate State Through Hearing." The text tells us it is called this "because even those who have committed the five boundless sins are sure to be liberated if they hear [*The Tibetan Book of the Dead*] by the path of the ear. Therefore read it in the midst of vast congregations. Disseminate it.... [I]t should be proclaimed in the ears of all living persons; it should be read over the pillows of all persons who are ill; it should be read at the side of all corpses: it should be spread broadcast."

As the deceased travels in bardo, she's urged by the lamas reading from the teaching to see the nature of reality and free herself from the *samsara* cycle of life, death, and rebirth. At the moment of death, she's "set face to face" with "the Clear Light of Reality," or the awakened mind. Should she fail to recognize it, she continues on in bardo, with chances throughout to attain liberation. If she doesn't seize these opportunities, she is reborn in one of six realms ranging from god to human to hell being.

I knew that *The Tibetan Book of the Dead* was also for the living, but I'd never quite grasped what this meant. Now, as my family members and I listened to the lamas encourage my grandmother to acknowledge that her old life had ended, I saw how their urgings could help us accept she was gone and let go of the life we'd had with her. We could also reflect on whether reluctance to face the truth—in our relationships, our jobs, our health—was hindering us on our bardo journey from birth to death.

As the funeral rites proceeded, a lama carried out a ritual cleansing by pouring saffron water on my grandmother's face. The coffin was brought up to the altar room and we threw in fragrant juniper sprigs as an offering to the deities while my grandmother's helper of fifty years, a diminutive Nepali woman with a long braid down her back, spritzed in the Elizabeth Arden perfume my grandmother loved.

My mother, a cousin, and I washed my grandmother's body with damp cloths. When someone dies, rigor mortis usually sets in, but her body remained supple, which was said to be a sign of advanced spiritual awareness. We exchanged her nightgown for an elegant burgundy *chuba* dress, because she had adored beauty and fashion. (When my daughter was born, my grandmother dispatched two gold baby bangles by express mail to Tokyo, for her "first, would-to-be-very-great, great-granddaughter.")

More condolence callers came with incense and khada scarves, and my grandmother's body was lifted into the coffin. Some relatives arrived with their young daughter, who wore a frilly pink dress. She waited excitedly to offer her khada, telling us, "When the lamas see me, they're going to say, 'Wow!'"

At midday, the family gathered in the dining room for momos, beef with cauliflower, and sweet oranges. The talk was of an impending strike, the heavy mist delaying flights from Calcutta, a Scottish guest at the hotel come to find out more about her father, who had attended St. Paul's School—alma mater of famed mountaineer Tenzing Norgay—and then fought the Japanese in Burma. "What is your life like in Japan?" everyone wanted to know. "What is the Japanese character?"

My grandmother's helper set aside a bit of the lunch food and, one last time, put it on a tray next to my grandmother's body, with the glass of hot water my grandmother enjoyed at meals. She then mixed some of the food with *tsampa* barley flour and spread it on hot coals outside, calling my grandmother's name so that no other spirit partook of the essences in the smoke. While some family members went for a rest and others continued listening to the lamas, I helped my mother put money into envelopes to be sent to the local monasteries, asking them to pray for my grandmother. Like this, on what for many was just another day in Darjeeling—children taking pony rides in Chowrasta, tourists bargaining for carpets and shawls in the bazaar—we prepared to say farewell.

The next morning dawned sunny and cloudless, a half-moon floating in the sky. It was the kind of day Tibetans consider auspicious, a sign that my grandmother would have a good rebirth. In the altar room, the final condolence callers came as the lamas packed up. Exactly at 9 a.m., male relatives lifted the coffin onto their shoulders and carried it out. Two lamas walked behind playing small *gyaling* horns, and the mournful bagpipe sound reverberated through the house.

For me, this was the saddest moment: My grandmother was leaving the place where she'd lived for over half a century. "Why not move somewhere less old-fashioned?" my mother often asked her. But my grandmother insisted on staying, not only because she loved her "lucky, darling" home, but because if she no longer lived there, who would light the butter lamps in the altar room for her father and her husband?

I tried not to cry as we descended the stairs, knowing my grandmother wouldn't have wanted me to. The tears of the surviving relatives are said to rain down on the dead person like hailstones; the family's sadness tethers her to this world because she doesn't want to leave them to their grief. "No relative or fond mate should be allowed to weep or to wail," *The Tibetan Book of the Dead* instructs, "as such is not good for the deceased; so restrain them." During my grandfather's last moments, my grandmother had made sure not to cry. Wanting him to begin his bardo journey in a peaceful state of mind, she stayed by his side and showed him photos from their golden anniversary celebration, when the family had gathered in London and seen Yul Brynner in *The King and I*.

My grandmother's coffin was put into a white Land Cruiser festooned with marigolds and we set off for Ghoom Monastery, where for over a hundred years our family had prayed and our dead had been cremated. When my great-grandfather died, his biography, *A Man of the Frontier*, reports, "his funeral...was held with full Police honours [and] was the largest ever seen in Darjeeling, with the cortege [to Ghoom] stretching for well over a mile."

Now the funeral procession for my grandmother along the same route caused a huge traffic jam. Drivers blasted their horns, leaned out their windows, and climbed on top of their vehicles to see what was happening. As the train chugged past on its way up from the plains, passengers pressed to the windows.

It took more than an hour for us to reach the town of Ghoom, usually a fifteen-minute journey. Finally, we turned off the main road into the narrow street leading to the monastery. People watched from houses and market stalls; dogs chased our cars, barking and leaping.

In my many years of visiting Ghoom Monastery, I'd rarely seen it in its entirety, because it was almost always shrouded in mist (some of us in the younger generation called it "Gloom"). But as my mother and I got out of the car, the bright saffron, red, and sapphire building appeared in full view: the big prayer wheels set into the outer walls; golden deer on the roof flanking the Wheel of Dharma, symbolizing the Buddha's first teaching at a deer park in Sarnath.

One of the lamas blew a conch shell, and then Rinpoche, the chief lama, led us once around the monastery, holding a khada scarf tied to the coffin to say to my grandmother, *Come this way.* He was her spiritual friend, guiding her with the bardo teachings in death as in life. Without such a friend, it was like being in an unpiloted boat—you couldn't cross the great river of samsara suffering to enlightenment.

Together with elderly Tibetan women singing ancient hymns and chanting prayers, we followed Rinpoche down a dirt track behind the monastery to the cremation ground. The coffin was placed on a pyre in a small pavilion crowned with a statue of the Buddha. Nearby, tall white prayer flags inscribed with mantras and wind horses fluttered in the breeze, the horses carrying the prayers out into the world to benefit all sentient beings.

Wearing dark sunglasses, her face solemn, my mother lit the pyre. Then it was my turn to touch a burning stick to the wood. The moments as the flames leaped up were calm and beautiful, just like my grandmother when she was dying. For three weeks, she sat on the veranda looking out over the houses and shops of the town that had been her home for almost a century, where she and my grandfather had gotten married in 1930 with "champagne and many layers of wedding cake" given to hundreds of guests, she often told me, and where her five children were born.

My grandmother lived her last days as she'd lived her other days, accepting the fleeting nature of life without regret. She was intimately acquainted with impermanence, not only because of her Buddhist faith but because of everything she'd experienced: Her parents, her six brothers, her husband, and most of her friends were dead; her children had all left India for good. As my mother and her siblings came of age, my grandparents hoped at least one of them would stay in Darjeeling, but "nothing doing," my grandmother said. When my mother married and settled in America, my grandfather grieved for a long time. My grandmother would find him looking at photos of my mother and wiping away tears. "You're just ruining your health," she said to him. "It's her life she's got to live. We're not going to live for her and we're not going to live forever!"

The flames rose higher and higher. Soon the coffin burned away and we could see my grandmother's charred body. Thick, black smoke drifted over the emerald tea gardens sloping down into the valleys, and far above, Kanchenjunga rose colossal and dreamlike in the turquoise sky.

Seated to one side of the pavilion, the lamas chanted and threw offerings on the pyre to benefit my grandmother in her next incarnation: incense for a long life, mustard seeds for protection from bad luck, black cumin for removal of sins, twigs for a good heart. We watched, talking quietly and drinking milky tea. An eagle soared high above the pyre, circling around and around, and everybody said this was lucky, a sign that my grandmother had set off well in bardo.

It took most of the day and night for my grandmother's body to burn. In the morning, the ash collector came and looked through the ashes. One of the lamas prayed over them, seeking indications of what kind of rebirth my grandmother would have. "In the case of an auntie," my grandmother once told me, "the lama saw a footprint, like of a bird, then one of a human, which meant before she took a human rebirth, she'd be reborn as a bird." When a high lama was cremated, jewellike relics were found in the ashes—indicating he had reached enlightenment—and kept as objects of worship.

In a convoy of Jeeps and Land Cruisers, we headed to the Teesta River to scatter my grandmother's ashes, just as had been done for my grandfather and other family members. As we drove down the winding road, past the villages and forests, the cold Himalayan air soon gave way to the warmth of the plains. At the Teesta, we stood together on the rocky bank and threw my grandmother's ashes into the blue-green water, to be carried away by the holy river to the sea.

## MY GRANDMOTHER'S FUNERAL

It's late March 2005, a few months after my grandmother's death, on what would have been her hundredth birthday. Three generations have gathered by the Teesta for a final ceremony to say goodbye to my grandmother. Aunts, uncles, brothers, sisters, cousins, grandchildren, great-grandchildren, we're all here, from London, Toronto, San Francisco, Tokyo, Bangkok, Colombo. The adults chat and gaze up at birds wheeling in the overcast sky as the children chase each other about. On the far side of the river, a gray crane stands motionless in the shallows, nearly invisible against the dark green of the trees.

Rinpoche walks along the bank, his red robe flapping in the breeze. He finds a spot where the water is clear and the current strong and sets out the ritual items: a hand bell, a butter lamp, and a prayer book. He arranges small pieces of wood, lights a fire, and tosses in juniper, then takes a seat on a rug. For an hour, he prays, swaying back and forth, his deep voice mingling with the sound of the flowing water, the cries of the birds.

After my grandmother's cremation, her bones were crushed and mixed with tsampa barley flour. Now, I crouch by the fire with family members and shape the tsampa into balls for the fish to eat. A few rays of sun break through the clouds as, one by one, we pick up a tsampa ball and throw it into the river, calling out my grandmother's name. It's my mother's turn, then mine. The tsampa balls arc high through the air and drop into the water, turning and returning in the cycle of life.

I feel the wind on my face, the passage of the days and years, of the river flowing to the sea. I watch the water stream past on its journey from the Himalayas to the Bay of Bengal and feel the great bloodlines coursing seaward from the Tibetan Plateau—the Mekong, the Yangtze, the Brahmaputra—their primeval, ceaseless current like the flow of the blood of the ancestors. I think about my grandmother journeying through the after-death bardo just as our ancestors did, about how, in the bardo between birth and death, I'm taking our story and mine forward, exploring the question that the ancient bardo teachings illuminate for our lives today:

*In a world where nothing lasts forever, how do we live?*

# 2.
# TIBET TO INDIA TO CALIFORNIA

This book is sent forth to the world in the hope that it may contribute something to the sum total of Right Knowledge,... binding East and West together in mutual respect and understanding.
—W. Y. Evans-Wentz, ed.,
*The Tibetan Book of the Dead*

[*The Tibetan Book of the Dead*] has got an incredible punch.... It's confrontational, and also a how-to guide.
—Laurie Anderson

Imagine Guru Rinpoche seated in splendid brocade robes atop a rocky promontory in the hills surrounding Lhasa, the sun blazing and the wind driving fleecy clouds ever higher in the deep blue sky. His wild-eyed, fierce countenance is still as he composes the bardo teachings. Beside him, Yeshe Tsogyal, a scholar and spiritual adept considered to be a female Buddha, transcribes the teachings, her crown glittering in the golden light. At Guru Rinpoche's behest, she will conceal the *Bardo Thödol* and other manuscripts in plants and trees, caves and lakes, dreams and the minds of future sages, to be revealed to coming generations.

According to legend, the bardo teachings are among the *terma*, or treasure texts, transmitted by Guru Rinpoche (also known as the Second Buddha and Padmasambhava) in the eighth century. A translation of his biography by my great-grandfather, S. W. Laden La, tells us that a large number of the terma "were written on tala-palm leaves, on silk, and on blue or lacquered paper in ink of gold, silver, copper, iron, and malachite, and enclosed in gold-lined boxes, earthen pots, stone receptacles, skulls, and precious stones." Among them are "five very rare essences of secret doctrines, the sacred books of Buddhism...and books on medicine, astrology, arts, and crafts."

In the fourteenth century, Karma Lingpa, a *tertön* discoverer of treasure texts, unearthed the bardo terma in a cave on a mountain in central Tibet. This makes it sound like the terma were dug out with a shovel, but the belief is that Karma Lingpa was able to locate them in a sacred geography accessible to him because of his special powers. At the time, a spiritual flowering was taking place in Tibet, and bardo teachings were spreading throughout the country in different versions according to the various Buddhist lineages. The scriptures revealed by Karma Lingpa would become known as the *Bardo Thödol*, and a selection of them would be published in 1927 by Oxford University Press as *The Tibetan Book of the Dead*.

The book's journey from its myth-shrouded origins to a London publishing house began on a rainy day in 1919, when W. Y. Evans-Wentz walked a winding mountain path from Darjeeling to Gangtok, Sikkim, in northeastern India. An American scholar and spiritual adventurer born in New Jersey and educated at Stanford and Oxford, Evans-Wentz was seeking to translate the *Bardo Thödol*. Carrying manuscripts that he'd purchased in Darjeeling and a letter of introduction from my great-grandfather, he was on his way to meet Lama Kazi Dawa-Samdup, the headmaster of a Gangtok school and a well-known translator. They began working together and—with Dawa-Samdup translating and Evans-Wentz editing—completed the first English translation of the *Bardo Thödol*, twelve centuries after the texts were composed by Guru Rinpoche.

No record exists of the initial encounter between Evans-Wentz and my great-grandfather, but it might be that they met at one of the teas Laden La hosted at his house down near the bazaar. Darjeeling was a thriving crossroads of Europeans, Anglo-Indians, Tibetans, Sikkimese, Nepalis, Bhutanese, and Bengalis, with local and national dignitaries, as well as visitors from abroad, passing through, and my great-grandfather's place was constantly abuzz.

"How many people came to tea!" my grandmother liked to remember. "The senior officer and his junior officer, viceroys, rajas and ranis, ambassadors. Big people, short people, mad people." There were scones and finger sandwiches and butterfly cakes arrayed on tiered stands, bearers in starched white jackets pouring Darjeeling's finest from gleaming silver teapots, and, always, much impassioned discussion, because my great-grandfather was deeply involved in political affairs. A diplomat as well as a police officer, he served as liaison for the Thirteenth Dalai Lama in 1910 when His Holiness took refuge in Darjeeling after the Chinese invaded Tibet. Two years later, my great-grandfather helped negotiate the withdrawal of the Chinese troops so the Dalai Lama could return home to Lhasa, and he was a key figure in the movement for the recognition of Darjeeling as a separate region from the province of Bengal, inspired, perhaps, by the campaign for Indian independence that was gaining momentum under the leadership of Mahatma Gandhi.

Or it might be that Evans-Wentz and Laden La became acquainted at a gathering one morning of the General Buddhist Association, started in 1907 by my great-grandfather, who was a devout Buddhist. Small in stature but with a vigorous, regal manner, Laden La strode smartly to the podium in traditional Tibetan dress and gave a talk on the nature of the mind. Seated in the back, Evans-Wentz, also in Tibetan dress, listened with rapt attention and came up afterward to introduce himself, mention his interest in translating the *Bardo Thödol*, and ask for elucidation of a few points in my great-grandfather's speech.

Laden La would have been happy to oblige—he knew the classic Buddhist texts well and spread the teachings in whatever ways he could. Orphaned at a young age, he had trained as a novice monk and continued his religious education after being adopted by an aunt and her husband, an eminent lama. With his Buddhist studies, Laden La was carrying forward both his Tibetan cultural inheritance and a family legacy: In the eighteenth century, one of our ancestors, Lama Rinzing Dorji Laden La, had founded a monastery in Darjeeling.

Having been tutored in the *Bardo Thödol* as well as heard it read many times—including when his wife died in 1911 and his adoptive father in 1915—my great-grandfather would have been keen to see Guru Rinpoche's masterwork translated so it could be shared with a larger readership. The book was of tremendous importance in Tibetan culture, as a guide not only for navigating the after-death bardo, but also for cultivating awareness and compassion in the bardo of this life, on the journey from birth to death.

Laden La was dedicated to Guru Rinpoche's teachings. As Evans-Wentz would later note in *The Tibetan Book of the Great Liberation*, which includes my great-grandfather's translation of Guru Rinpoche's biography, he "was one of the really true Buddhists of our generation.... Of the Great [Guru Rinpoche] he was a fervent devotee."

Every year, my great-grandfather led a group of local Buddhists on pilgrimage to Tso Pema, a lake in northern India where, legend says, Guru Rinpoche performed miracles. Departing Darjeeling in the predawn hours with bedding, pots and pans, and a churner to make butter tea ("The Indians used to ask, 'What is that you all are carrying?'" my grandmother told me. "'A Tibetan cannon?'"), Laden La and his party traveled nearly a thousand miles to the sacred lake. On the surface of the water was an island of reeds. "If you are a good religious person," my grandmother said, "the island moves in the direction of your arrival to greet you. It always floated toward my father as he approached."

My great-grandfather's faith in Guru Rinpoche was no doubt strengthened by a near-death experience he had in 1912. While riding his pony down from Tibet after negotiating the withdrawal of the Chinese troops, he was caught in an avalanche and buried along with many of the men in his party, their ponies, and their mules. Somehow, he was able to thrust his arm through the snow. He waved his rosary back and forth, praying, "Save me, Guru Rinpoche! Save me!" Someone saw him and he was rescued.

That day, my great-grandfather put into practice a central lesson of the bardo teachings: Accept the reality of your situation, but don't give up. If he'd fallen into denial and wasted precious minutes telling himself that things weren't that dire, or wishing he were riding along as usual on a sunny morning in the Himalayas, he would have perished. For him, the *Bardo Thödol* was not only a religious text but a manual for everyday existence that guided his thoughts and actions—and saved his life.

~

After completing the translation of the *Bardo Thödol* with Dawa-Samdup, Evans-Wentz took the manuscript to England, and *The Tibetan Book of the Dead* was published on August 12, 1927. It awakened a fascination in the West with the bardo teachings as both a primer on the mystery of death and a handbook for living. Celebrated by luminaries ranging from Carl Jung to Timothy Leary to Laurie Anderson to George Saunders, the book has sold over a million copies, including subsequent translations, and is still in print today. How did it achieve such broad and lasting renown?

"It's difficult to know just what audience Evans-Wentz had in mind when he finally presented his [translation] to Oxford University Press," Ken Winkler says in *Pilgrim of the Clear Light*, his biography of Evans-Wentz. "The reading public was quite different in the 1920s, and the popularization of Eastern spirituality had yet to transpire."

The book's esoteric ideas, volume of material, and archaic language made it unlikely to appeal to more than a handful of scholars of Buddhism and Tibet. Though the death-to-rebirth journey was commonly accepted among Tibetans, the concept would have appeared fantastical to most westerners, especially because of the way in which it's described. The text explains the after-death bardo voyage as divided into three main parts: *Chikhai*, the moment of death, when the Clear Light of Reality (the awakened mind) dawns; *Chönyid*, when karmically induced hallucinations appear in the form of forty-two peaceful and fifty-eight wrathful deities, representing our innate wisdom; and *Sidpa*, when we come up for judgment in the court of Yama, Lord of Death, and the world of our rebirth is decided. At any point, we're told, we can embrace the true nature of our mind and attain liberation.

Included in the translation were prayers and mantras, guidelines for the lamas reading the book aloud ("If there be no corpse, then the bed or the seat to which the deceased had been accustomed should be occupied by the reader, who ought to expound the power of the Truth"), and instructions to the deceased ("O nobly-born, from the west will dawn the Greenish-Black Vulture-Headed Eater-Goddess... fear that not"). There was also a foreword by Sir John Woodroffe ("late a Judge of the High Court, Calcutta, now Reader in Indian Law in the University of Oxford"), with sections such as "Reincarnation v. Resurrection," "Consciousness Transference," and "Continuity of Transformation," as well as a preface, an extensive introduction, detailed footnotes, an appendix, and addenda contributed by Evans-Wentz.

Whatever Evans-Wentz had in mind when he brought the book to Oxford University Press, he surely never dreamed that it would ignite an enduring passion in the West for the bardo teachings. He couldn't have imagined it would give rise to a global conversation about Buddhism and personal development, appealing to generations of scholars and scientists, spiritual explorers and hospice movement advocates, hippies and artists, who were eager to not only learn more about death, but to live life with greater meaning and authenticity.

In a lengthy "Psychological Commentary" that appeared in the third edition of *The Tibetan Book of the Dead* (1960), Swiss psychologist Carl Jung wrote, "The Bardo Thödol... caused a considerable stir in English-speaking countries at the time of its first appearance in 1927. It belongs to that class of writings which are not only of interest to specialists in Mahāyāna Buddhism, but which also, because of their deep humanity and their still deeper insight into the secrets of the human psyche, make an especial appeal to the layman who is seeking to broaden his knowledge of life."

Embracing the book as a map to self-realization, Jung continued, "For years, ever since it was first published, the *Bardo Thödol* has been my constant companion, and to it I owe not only many stimulating ideas and discoveries, but also many fundamental insights."

One reason for the popularity of *The Tibetan Book of the Dead* is that it speaks to the impulse Jung identified: our urge to seek greater meaning in life. Often seen as a quest narrative, where we are the heroes, the book resonates with the story of the Buddha and his search for enlightenment; with the *Odyssey*, the *Divine Comedy*, and *The Canterbury Tales*; *Don Quixote*, *The Pilgrim's Progress*, and *Ulysses*. In 1964, counterculture icon Timothy Leary, along with Richard Alpert (Ram Dass) and Ralph Metzner, published *The Psychedelic Experience: A Manual Based on the Tibetan Book of the Dead*, a pocket reference for traveling through "interior territories" to "liberation, illumination, or enlightenment" with the aid of LSD-25, mescaline, and psilocybin. Thirty years later, in his own translation of the *Bardo Thödol*, Buddhist scholar and former Tibetan monk Robert Thurman noted—echoing Jung ("an especial appeal to the layman")—the wisdom that *The Tibetan Book of the Dead* offers to "those of us unable to reach the heights of [adept Lamas]," explaining that the teaching "can be used by any seeker in any [tradition] for its systematic technologies and its penetrating insight."

The book also fascinates as a guide to coming to terms with the inevitability of death. This is seen, for example, in a 1994 Japanese-French-Canadian documentary, *The Tibetan Book of the Dead: A Way of Life*, which explores death as universal and the bardo teachings as an essential guide to confronting our mortality. Narrated by singer and poet Leonard Cohen, the film opens with bardo rituals being performed in Ladakh, India, for an old man who has passed away. "O son of noble family, now is the time for you to seek a path," says the *ngakpa*, or Buddhist yogi, seated next to the corpse and reading from *The Tibetan Book of the Dead*. "You are not alone in leaving this world. Everyone who has come before you has died."

The documentary then takes us thousands of miles around the globe to San Francisco, home of the Living/Dying Project, an organization that supports the dying as they journey from life to death. We see a staff member talking with a terminally ill man about death and later reading to him from *The Tibetan Book of the Dead*: "Listen to what I am saying, Bruce. Death has now come and you are departing from this world, but you are not the only one, as death comes to all people on earth." The wisdom of *The Tibetan Book of the Dead*, the film says, helps us to be more accepting of the law of impermanence, no matter who we are or where we live.

The book offers guidance and solace in the face of the frightening reality that one day, we will cease to be. The attraction of the teachings as a salve for our fear of death is addressed by the Dalai Lama in his foreword to *The Tibetan Book of the Dead: First Complete Translation* (2005), a 535-page tome "composed by Padmasambhava, revealed by Terton Karma Lingpa, translated by Gyurme Dorje, edited by Graham Coleman with Thupten Jinpa, Introductory Commentary by His Holiness The Dalai Lama." His Holiness says, "A sense of uncertainty, and often fear, is a natural human feeling when thinking about the nature of death and the relationship between living and dying. It is perhaps not surprising therefore that...the *Tibetan Book of the Dead*, a treasure-text which focuses on this important subject, has become one of the best-known works of Tibetan literature in the West."

"Death cometh to all," *The Tibetan Book of the Dead* says, not only urging us to accept that death cannot be avoided, but reassuring us that impermanence is all right, an ordinary rather than exceptional phenomenon. The fact that everything and everyone we love, and we ourselves, will one day vanish may seem patently *not* all right, but the bardo teachings guide us in overcoming our terror and recognizing the possibilities available to us because we're human. As Evans-Wentz writes in his preface to the third edition of the book, the teachings help us "not to fritter away in the worthless doings of this world the supreme opportunity afforded by human birth."

In Buddhist belief, the chance of being born human is similar to the likelihood that a blind tortoise that rises to the surface of the ocean every one hundred years will put its head through a golden yoke drifting on the waves. If we're lucky enough to come into this world as a human (rather than, say, an ant or a tree), we possess the capacity to acknowledge our mortality and, spurred by this awareness, make the most of our lives.

Our intuition of this uniquely human power—together with the allure of between-states in both time and space—accounts in no small measure for the appeal of *The Tibetan Book of the Dead*. Liminality as transformation is imprinted on our psyche from an early age. Fairy tales are all about metamorphosis: After slumbering for a hundred years, Sleeping Beauty awakens; Hansel and Gretel defeat the witch in the forest and return home; Cinderella endures the cruel treatment of her stepmother and stepsisters and becomes a princess. Liminality as evolution is seen in the natural world: a caterpillar in its cocoon, a flower between bud and blossom. We experience it in the betweenness offered by travel: On a flight from somewhere to somewhere, changing planes in an unfamiliar city, we're untethered from our usual lives, anonymous, journeying in interstitial spaces that offer a chance for unaccustomed vistas, literally and figuratively.

Enchanted by what she observed from the plane on a journey around the world, to Japan and India, Syria and Iran, artist Georgia O'Keefe wrote to her sister while in flight, "Such things as I have seen out this window I have never dreamed...a great river system of green and grey seeming to run up hill to a most dream like lake of bluish and pinkish grey...then great areas of sand in soft dark wave like shapes."

The perspectives that air travel gave O'Keefe inspired her to paint works such as *Blue, Black and Grey* and *Green, Yellow and Orange*, in which sinuous lines and forms suggest rivers winding through landscapes, and *An Island with Clouds*, where white clouds float over a green island in a sea of blue. Her excitement—and the new, more abstract directions she took as an artist after she began traveling by plane—captures the sense of possibility, of becoming, inherent in the between.

Our fascination with between-states as transformative spaces is evident in three contemporary novels: George Saunders's *Lincoln in the Bardo* (2017), about Abraham Lincoln's grief over the death of his young son Willie and his eventual acceptance of the loss; Shehan Karunatilaka's *The Seven Moons of Maali Almeida* (2022), the story of a Sri Lankan photojournalist who is murdered during his country's civil war, wakes up in the "In Between," and, at first unwilling to admit he's dead, gradually comes to terms with his situation; and Lorrie Moore's *I Am Homeless If This Is Not My Home* (2023), in which a man undertakes a road trip with the corpse of his ex-girlfriend and finds insight into life.

Attraction to bardo as a site of awakening is also seen in recent music and film. In 2019, Laurie Anderson's *Songs from the Bardo*, recorded with Tenzin Choegyal and Jesse Paris Smith, was released; the songs include "Awakened One," "Brilliant Lights," and "Awakened Heart." The liner notes tell us that the songs on the album, which was nominated for a Grammy, relate to *The Tibetan Book of the Dead*'s "[aim] to help those whose consciousness has entered the intermediate state to move themselves into a new reality, with the ultimate goal of...[becoming] enlightened."

2022 brought Alejandro González Iñárritu's film *Bardo, False Chronicle of a Handful of Truths*, the story of a Mexican journalist who's been living in Los Angeles, returns to his home country, and gains new perspectives on his identity as he navigates a liminal space between the United States and Mexico. The process of making the film led Iñárritu to a fresh outlook on his own situation as a longtime resident of Los Angeles with a deep attachment to Mexico. He says, "What I've understood is there are no answers, there's no conclusion. All of us who have migrated should embrace the fact we do not belong, that we are becoming something.... I'm not solidly in one place, not intellectually, not spiritually, not physically, meaning I'm in permanent transformation."

From Saunders to Iñárritu, these examples show the groundbreaking possibilities that geographical, emotional, and psychological bardo between-states offer us.

Through the wisdom we gain in the between, be it a plane trip or a longer period, we can profoundly alter our path. In bardo, *The Tibetan Book of the Dead* tells us, "the intellect becometh ninefold more lucid"; in addition, "one possesseth the slender sense of supernormal perception and... the mind is capable of being changed or influenced." My own journey to *The Tibetan Book of the Dead* embodied this transformative possibility, not only bringing me to the bardo teachings but returning me to myself.

We experience between-states from a young age, times when our identity is in flux, whether it's our social identity, our sexual identity, our ethnic identity. Growing up in 1960s and 1970s suburban New Jersey and California, I felt this kind of liminality as one of the few Asian American kids in my neighborhood and, except for my three siblings, the only Tibetan American.

Determined that her children feel they belonged, and eager to plunge into the land of the free after her traditional upbringing in Darjeeling, my mother raised us *à la American*, as she liked to say. Instead of observing *Losar* Tibetan New Year and the *Saga Dawa* celebration of the Buddha's life, she went all-out on American holidays, organizing Easter egg hunts and tucking piles of presents under the Christmas tree with *from Santa C.* written on the tags. My intellectual American father—a psychiatrist, he majored in philosophy at Princeton, studied in Paris at the Sorbonne, and spent his free time reading Montaigne, Pascal, and Sartre—objected to my mother's activities as mindless obedience to social norms. But I sided with my mother, because I loved the egg hunts and presents and, best of all, no one would know I was half-Tibetan.

My plain vanilla name, Ann Davis, kept its secrets—sort of. Since I had olive skin and almond-shaped eyes, my classmates tried to guess my ethnicity: "Hawaiian? Irish? Italian?" If I revealed that I was born in Spain when my father was stationed at a naval base in Andalusia, the mystery was solved: "Oh, *Spanish.*" But the othering didn't end. One day on the playground in middle school, three boys linked arms and marched in circles around me, chanting *Ching, Chong, Chinaman! Ching, Chong, Chinaman!* It was clear that my mother's camouflage strategy—and therefore, I myself—was doomed, because I couldn't change how I looked.

At night, I lay awake wishing for blue eyes and blonde hair. I resolved never, ever, to divulge my Tibetan heritage.

Things would only get harder if my classmates discovered I wasn't Spanish or Chinese but had roots in some strange place they'd never heard of. "We will be pleased to meet your friends!" my sociable grandfather would say when he and my grandmother arrived from Darjeeling for a visit. I loved my grandparents, but I prayed we wouldn't run into anyone I knew at the Statue of Liberty or Ghirardelli Square or Lake Tahoe, my grandfather dapper in a three-piece suit and, worst of all, my grandmother in full Tibetan dress.

When adults found out about my Tibetan half, they'd tell me I was "exotic" and get excited in a New Age way. It was the era of flower power, the Human Be-In and Woodstock; personal transformation programs like EST and Esalen. Tibetan Buddhism was becoming popular: Lamas who had gone into exile in India and Nepal after the Chinese took over Tibet in 1959 were continuing on to the West, founding dharma centers and teaching Buddhism just as unconventional lifestyles and philosophies were entering the zeitgeist. Senior lamas who never would have come down from the Tibetan Plateau were living and teaching in Seattle, Berkeley, and other cities across America.

Only vaguely aware of the tenor of the times, I couldn't understand why people asked me about things like reincarnation if they found out my mother was Tibetan. I kept a low profile, studied French (inspired by my Francophile father), and spent a post-high-school gap year working as an au pair on the Left Bank, near the cafés frequented by writers I admired, like Hemingway and Joyce. Back in the United States for college, I studied French and Latin American literature and decided I would become a writer and live in Paris. Not only had I fallen in love with that beautiful city, but France felt reassuringly distant from America, where I still languished in the between—"American" on one side and "Tibetan" (whatever that was) on the other.

Although I tried to prepare for my move to Europe the summer after I graduated, I could hardly get through the day, much less launch a life abroad. I'd lost the divine structure of university, the haven where I could hole up in my carrel on the third basement floor of the library and lose myself in Flaubert and Proust and Stendhal, Cortázar and Borges and García Márquez. In the apartment I was renting with my boyfriend in Cambridge, Massachusetts, I'd lie in bed and wonder what was going to become of me.

Looking back now at that time, I realize that, from a young age, I hadn't been able to see my liminality, my racial and cultural heritage, as a gift. Instead, I'd tumbled along, as we so often do, in the currents of family and societal expectation—as a girl, trying to fit in; at college, choosing a major that I adored but that was far removed from my Asianness—unable to grasp that I could become anything I wanted. As the years passed, I perhaps sensed the possibilities of the between, and that wide openness is what I was avoiding because I couldn't figure out how to live into it.

For reasons I didn't understand, I abandoned my Paris dream and left Cambridge for Darjeeling, winging my way back like a homing pigeon to the place I'd last seen when I was three.

Visiting my mother's hometown after two decades, I felt like an archaeologist happening upon the excavation site I'd been searching for. I washed my face by candlelight in the bathroom my mother had used and slept in her old bed. In the afternoons, I talked with my grandmother over tea and heard about her time in Tibet in the 1920s, when she walked the pilgrimage route around the seventh-century Jokhang Temple in Lhasa and had an audience with the Thirteenth Dalai Lama at his Norbulingka Palace. She told me about her father's association with Evans-Wentz and *The Tibetan Book of the Dead*; my grandfather's early days as the son of a vegetable seller and how he had risen to be a magistrate and hotel owner; the winter morning when my mother, who was "very bold from childhood," waved a cheerful goodbye to her weeping parents and flew off to America.

In my grandmother's living room was an elephant's-foot stool, the only thing I remembered from when I was a little girl because I'd found it so impressive: the leopard-skin seat, the leathery gray hide, the big brown toenails. "That elephant," my grandmother recalled, "your great-grandfather shot. It was a rogue elephant. There was no such a person that elephant didn't attack." She liked to remember how, at the end of a long day, her father would come home and sit on the stool and they'd talk—about his work as a Darjeeling District police officer, his activities with local Buddhist organizations, his diplomatic efforts on the India-Tibet frontier. Then they'd go together to the altar room and pray to Guru Rinpoche.

As I heard my grandmother's stories, a world began to emerge, unfolding like the Japanese origami that Proust writes about in *Swann's Way*, the first volume of *In Search of Lost Time*. The adult protagonist tastes a crumb of *petite madeleine* dipped in tea, and his childhood universe in the village of Combray appears before him "as in that game enjoyed by the Japanese," where pieces of paper "until then indistinct" open out into "flowers, houses, human figures" when put in water. Listening to my grandmother's tales unlocked a door to my cultural memory. I began to conceive of myself as being part of a past and a future that encompassed my family, the Tibetan community in Darjeeling, and Tibet a few hundred miles to the north.

Inspired by my newfound sense of belonging, I spent afternoons at Darjeeling's Oxford Book and Stationery Co. perusing volumes on Buddhism and Tibet, among them *The Tibetan Book of the Dead*. I loved reading and rereading Evans-Wentz's acknowledgment of my great-grandfather in the preface: "Sardar Bahadur S.W. Laden La, Chief of Police, Darjeeling, who sent me to Gangtok with a letter of introduction to the late Lāma Kazi Dawa-Samdup, the translator of the *Bardo Thödol*."

I imagined my great-grandfather's delighted goodwill toward this American scholar with a passion for Buddhism who'd turned up one day in Darjeeling. Perhaps they had a look together at the very same bookshop shelves I was now exploring, Laden La introducing Evans-Wentz to publications of interest and the two of them conferring in low tones.

Besides being intrigued by our family's connection to *The Tibetan Book of the Dead*, I was attracted to the idea of between-states that held great potential for transformation. Perhaps, after wandering in the between for so many years, I'd found a way to become better at the navigation that life demands of us all. In the years to come, as I started my career, got married, and had children, my fascination with *The Tibetan Book of the Dead* as a part of my family legacy and a guide to forging our path would never waver.

One of the objects I inherited from my grandmother is a faded red Tibetan saddle rug that belonged to my great-grandfather. On the front is an intricate mandala pattern, and on the back, his initials: S.W.L. I like to think this is the rug he used when he rode his pony to Tibet, traveling for weeks across the vast plateau in company with herds of deer and gazelle that stretched for miles, caravans carrying tea and jewels and perfumes down to Nepal and India, explorers seeking the source of the great rivers. I see him crossing fifteen-thousand-foot Jelep Pass, the sun shining and the wind gusting. He throws his arms in the air and calls out, "Kyi kyi so so lha gyal lo!" (*May the gods win!*), a traditional prayer for safe passage, an acknowledgment that we are travelers in bardo, a shout of joy and gratitude for this life.

Sharing the bardo teachings with you, I feel I'm continuing my great-grandfather's work, especially now as the hundredth anniversary of the publication of *The Tibetan Book of the Dead* approaches. We're only passing through as we travel from birth to death, but the journey, guided by the wisdom of the teachings, offers riches beyond what we dream possible.

# 3.
# COMING TO REALIZE YOU ARE DEAD

"So-and-so, listen. You are dead, be sure of that. You have nothing more to do here. Eat copiously for the last time. You have a long road to run and several mountain passes to cross. Take strength and do not return ever again."

—Alexandra David-Néel,
*Magic and Mystery in Tibet*


We don't have to fear change, what is other shouldn't frighten us.

—Elena Ferrante

A fundamental part of the bardo journey is realizing you are dead. (I felt puzzled when I first heard this: How can we recognize that we're dead… if we're dead?) It's believed that the dead linger for up to about four days, calling out to their loved ones, "Why so sad? I'm right over here!" *The Tibetan Book of the Dead* tells us, "When the consciousness-principle getteth outside the body, it sayeth to itself, 'Am I dead, or am I not dead?' It cannot determine. It seeth its relatives and connexions as it had been used to seeing them before. It even heareth the wailings."

There are stories of people who, in desperation, endeavor to reenter their bodies. "A man we knew wanted to go back into his body," my grandmother told me, remembering a funeral she attended in Tibet in 1924. "We couldn't see him but the high lama there saw that the dead man was trying to bring the corpse again to life."

"O nobly-born, that which is called death hath now come," *The Tibetan Book of the Dead* says, urging us to accept that the existence we've known is over. Our reluctance to face endings is normal, in that it's quintessentially human. We're wired to shy away from the unfamiliar and cling to what we know, driven by what essayist Maria Popova calls "a reptilian dread that plays out with the same ferocity on scales personal, societal, and civilizational." It's easy to imagine cave dwellers feeling anxious about change: Even if your cave had become virtually unlivable, venturing out into unaccustomed territory could mean finding yourself in a cave that was worse than the one you had, being attacked by a hostile tribe or caught unawares by a woolly mammoth.

Although our aversion to change might feel like a Darwinian optimization of our chances of survival, it can hinder the flourishing of our mind and spirit, the living of a meaningful life in a world where—as the Buddha taught thousands of years ago—impermanence is the only thing we can be sure of. In this sense, accepting change is essential to our survival. Though we may feel that change puts us at risk, from a Buddhist perspective it's not change that threatens us but our resistance to it.

~

Are you clinging to a relationship that's finished? Wasting time in a job that's grown pointless? Denying your parents' aging and mortality? Holding on to a belief system or way of living that no longer serves you? *The Tibetan Book of the Dead* invites us to recognize the many kinds of death that can occur in the midst of our lives.

Perhaps your marriage is over, but you're telling yourself *it's just a bump in the road, all couples go through ups and downs*. You yearn for the relationship you once had, reminiscing about the good old days, and at the same time assure yourself that tomorrow will be different, even though it never is. "You know, when there's a noise breaking into your sleep and you don't want to wake up, you can dream a long, complicated dream that explains the noise away," Amy Witting writes in her novel *A Change in the Lighting*, the story of a woman who has been holding on to her marriage even though it's fallen apart. Wandering in the labyrinth of a dream, we refuse to admit that our relationship has come to an end.

We may also resist the truth when our jobs lose meaning. Bored and on autopilot, you quiet quit, unwilling to accept that your job is no longer right for you and maybe never was. You blind yourself to your situation, telling yourself *every job has its disadvantages, switching careers will put me in a shaky financial position, it's too late to start something new.*

As the COVID-19 pandemic brought an end to work, school, family, and social life as we knew it, and sickened and killed millions, many of us plunged into denial. We tried to convince ourselves that the medical community was overreacting, the research "wasn't there yet," COVID was just another kind of flu. Loath to face the reality that was unfolding, we fantasized about returning to our previous existence.

We may, to our surprise, grapple with eagerly anticipated transitions, such as moving or having a baby. However much we've looked forward to the next stage in our lives, the end of the reality we've known can trigger a debilitating longing for the past. Freshly arrived in an unfamiliar city, you might find that nostalgia for your old home—family and friends, favorite shops and restaurants—is keeping you from embracing the present. With a new baby, you may crave time alone, late nights out, an uninterrupted meal, a shower, or more sleep; you wish for the days when your time was your own and no one depended on you 24/7 for their survival.

Another kind of ending that we turn away from is the loss of a pet. I struggled to accept what was happening as my Westie, Mac, grew old. I began to notice signs when he was about fifteen: He didn't hear me approaching, he lost his balance and tumbled down the stairs, his legs became stiff. If we continued giving him plenty of exercise every day, I reasoned, the stiffness would get better. Dogs sometimes lived to eighteen or twenty, why not Mac?

My denial and sadness were intensified because our nest was now empty, and Mac's imminent death was intertwined with the end of my children's childhood. I would find him in their bedrooms, fast asleep amid the stuffed animals and board games and high school yearbooks. I'd put my hand on his chest to feel his heart beat and wonder: Did he have another week? A month? A year?

One day, I took him to the veterinarian for a checkup. "Mondai nai, right?" I said as the vet studied the results of a blood test. This had been our conversation for years, whenever Mac had an ailment, and I expected the doctor would again agree that everything was going to be fine.

He shook his head. "Mondai aru." *There's a problem.*

The end came about six months later, when I was traveling abroad with my son, Henry. My husband, David, emailed and said that Mac's kidneys were failing and he was in pain, that the vet was recommending we let him go. Still, I thought Mac could carry on a bit longer—this was just a rough patch. As soon as I got back to Tokyo, I'd look into the latest medications and therapies and find the best treatment for him.

The day before I returned, David called, Mac panting in his arms, and said we couldn't wait any longer. Henry and I were with them on FaceTime as they rode in a taxi to the veterinary clinic. Before the doctor administered the shot, I thanked him for taking good care of Mac for sixteen years. "Let him sleep now," he said. David, Henry, and I wept as we saw the light go out of Mac's eyes. The vet and his assistant bowed their heads and said a prayer.

Hard as it is to face the death of a pet, we're also confronted by the far greater challenge of watching the people we love grow old. As my mother ages, I find myself resisting her decline, clinging to who she used to be.

The first Tibetan to attend medical school in America, my mother was a brilliant doctor. In her late eighties, she came to stay for a week at the East Village loft I was renting, and I organized a dinner, knowing how she adores a party (vice president of her Columbia class, she was known as the "president of vice," throwing bashes where, she liked to tell me, they "drank loads of sake and rumbaed down the hall!").

That evening, my mother excused herself early, saying she was exhausted. I accompanied her to the bedroom, trying to persuade her to stay longer, but she lay down and closed her eyes, murmuring, "It's a lovely party. You go ahead and enjoy it." I sat in the dark and stared out at the glittering lights of the city, fighting dread. My mother was just tired after the flight from San Francisco. In the morning, she'd be back to her fun-loving self, and we'd catch an exhibit at the Met, go shopping at Bloomingdale's, pop over to Jackson Heights for momos. I told myself this even though the indications she was slowing down had been there for a while. She'd started falling, misplacing things, telling me that important matters needed to be taken care of but not being sure what they were, calling me from her retirement home to say she was lost and to please come for her immediately. The signs were clear, yet I clung to my mother as I'd known her.

The sudden loss of someone we love can also throw us into denial. Joan Didion writes about this in *The Year of Magical Thinking*, her memoir about the year after her husband's death. One evening, her husband suffered a fatal heart attack as they were sitting down to dinner. "John was talking," Didion says, "then he wasn't." Sorting through

John's clothes after he's gone, she's unable to give away all of his shoes, imagining he'll need some if he comes back.

When my father died unexpectedly, I experienced a similar feeling. He'd contracted sepsis and fallen into a coma in the space of a day; the doctors said there was no chance of recovery and doubted I'd make it to California from Tokyo in time to say goodbye. I'd read somewhere that hearing is the last sense to go, so I asked my sisters to tell my father I was on my way. As I ran out the door to catch the train to Narita Airport, I threw the latest *Le Monde diplomatique* into my bag. It was my father's favorite newspaper, and I'd picked it up at the bookstore earlier that week to send to him as usual.

When I arrived at Queen of the Valley Medical Center in Napa, my father was still in a coma, but he'd waited for me, as I'd known he would. I sat by his side and began reading to him from *Le Monde diplomatique*. We loved discussing all things French, from philosophy to politics to food, and now, I was certain, he would wake as he heard about *l'arabe, une "langue de France" sacrifiée* and *les révolutions de Rousseau*. He'd open his eyes and we'd talk: What was the relationship between French constitutional principles of secularism and the failure to teach Arabic, the country's second most widely spoken language, at more French secondary schools? What effect did the ideas of Jean-Jacques Rousseau have on revolutions in Latin America and Asia, not to mention the United States? Rousseau's tomb was in the Panthéon, my father would tell me; when he was studying at the Sorbonne, he went to see it one rainy April afternoon after class and then met his girlfriend for an apéro at Café Le Rostand by the Jardin du Luxembourg. I'd tell him about the friend I caught up with at Le Rostand when I was last in Paris, how she had five children and worked as an editor, and he'd ask about my views on women's status in French society; we'd mull over how the situation for women might change since Hollande had defeated Sarkozy in the recent presidential election.

But my father didn't wake, and less than an hour after I arrived, he died.

My sisters and I fluttered around him, stroking his hands and face, as if to imprint his corporeality on our own. Phone calls were made, someone handed me a "Bereavement Packet," there was talk of an autopsy (complete or partial, brain-only, tissue procurement), a man in a black suit came from the mortuary and arrangements were decided.

As I drove away, turning south on Route 29, the harvest moon rose above the mountains to the east. Blue twilight sifted down over the vineyards, just like when my father visited me during my year in France and we motored along the roads of Provence, twilight falling over the lavender fields. Surely we would take a trip like that again.

A few days after my father's death, I returned home to Tokyo, carrying some of his favorite possessions for safekeeping, things I'd hold on to for him because what if he wanted them later? A striped button-down shirt; *Paris des rêves* (*Paris of Dreams*), a book of black-and-white photographs and poems given to him by his French girlfriend; his well-worn copy of *Essais* by sixteenth-century philosopher Michel de Montaigne; the binoculars he used when we went bird-watching in the Marin Headlands near San Francisco. The objects seemed animated by his life force—if they still existed, why, in some way he must too. For almost a year I struggled to accept he was gone, unable to mourn as I clung to the idea that I'd see him again.

Our all-too-human inclination to resist sudden endings is explored in George Saunders's and Shehan Karunatilaka's bardo-related novels. In Saunders's *Lincoln in the Bardo*, President Lincoln clings to his son Willie after the boy dies of typhoid fever, visiting the crypt again and again to take Willie's corpse from the coffin and hold it on his lap. Lingering in the after-death bardo, Willie is confident he'll be able to go back to his old life. "My mother," he tells his companions in the between. "My father. They will come shortly. To collect me." He's surrounded by dead people who are also denying the truth of their situation, such as Hans Vollman (killed by a falling beam), who's convinced he's only temporarily ill and will soon be returning to his wife.

In Karunatilaka's *The Seven Moons of Maali Almeida*, the murdered Sri Lankan photojournalist, Almeida, assures himself that the afterlife is just a dream he can soon exit. "I can't be here," he informs the woman at the reception counter. "I have photos to share. I'm in a committed relationship." Characters like these are a mirror for all of us as we hold on to fading relationships, old ways of life, and our loved ones, unwilling to accept the changes that have taken place.

*The Last White Man*, a novel by British-Pakistani writer Mohsin Hamid, is also about abrupt loss that's hard to accept. A white man, Anders, wakes up one day and discovers "he had turned a deep and undeniable brown"; longing to return to his previous existence, he struggles to come to terms with the end of the life he's known. In a conversation for my *Tricycle* magazine interview series about bardo, Hamid told me about his own experience of unexpected loss and offered striking insight. A graduate of Princeton University and Harvard Law School, he was working for a consulting company in London when the 9/11 attacks catapulted him out of the life he'd known as "a brown-skinned guy with a Muslim name" who was "reasonably unbothered" by discrimination. Suddenly, he was seen as a threat: He was pulled from airport lines and interrogated; people moved away from him when he got on the bus or walked into a room. He found he was stuck, unwilling to accept what had happened—or let himself grieve for what he had lost—and trying to reassure himself that he could return to the life he'd had. He explained,

"There's a spiritual kind of Wile E. Coyote phenomenon, where you've walked off the edge of the cliff and you think you're floating there, but you're really plummeting to the bottom of the valley."

⁓

To move forward, *The Tibetan Book of the Dead* tells us, we must face the truth of our situation and let go of whatever we're clinging to. When my grandmother died, the rituals that were carried out helped me understand how important the principle of nonattachment is to the bardo teachings.

Reading from *The Tibetan Book of the Dead*, the lamas encouraged my grandmother to accept her new reality:

> O this now is the hour of death.
> Do not cling, in fondness and weakness, to this life. Even though thou clingest out of weakness, thou hast not the power to remain here.
> Be not attached to this world.

Sometimes the exhortations during bardo rites reach even greater intensity. Journeying in Tibet in the 1920s, Alexandra David-Néel witnessed a funeral where a fictitious story was concocted to hasten the dead man on his way. In *Magic and Mystery in Tibet*, her book about her travels, she recounts what was said to the deceased, Pagdzin: "I must tell you that your house has been destroyed by a fire, everything you possessed is burned. Because of a debt you had forgotten, your creditor has taken your two sons away as slaves. Your wife has left with a new husband. As it would sadden you to see all this misery, be careful not to return." When David-Néel inquired if these calamities had indeed come to pass, she was told, "We invented [this] tale to disgust Pagdzin so that he will not think of returning to his home."

During a break in the rites for my grandmother, I chatted with Rinpoche, the head lama, and learned more about how attachment is viewed in Tibetan Buddhism. A compact, muscular man with a cheerful demeanor, he knew all too well about what it is to lose the life you've loved, having fled his homeland of Amdo in northeastern Tibet and followed the Dalai Lama into exile after the Chinese takeover. What's more, since high-ranking lamas are said to have gone through many deaths and rebirths, he was considered a seasoned bardo traveler, adept at nonclinging. "Attachment is the root cause of all suffering," he told me. "You can't take things with you, so why attach to them?"

On the fourth morning, the day of the cremation, one of the lamas wrapped the black end of a string around my grandmother's thumb and gave us the white end. With a small knife, he cut the string, severing my grandmother's attachment to this world and our attachment to her. When we arrived at Ghoom Monastery, Rinpoche stood for a moment next to the coffin, said some prayers, and then told my grandmother, "You are dead. Now you must go." He led us down the path to the cremation ground, holding the *khada* scarf tied to my grandmother's coffin. ("From time to time, the chief *lāma* looks back to invite the spirit to accompany the body," Evans-Wentz explains in his introduction to *The Tibetan Book of the Dead*, "and to assure it that the route is in the right direction.")

When the coffin was set on the stacked wood in the pavilion, I was startled to be handed the burning stick—I'd never imagined that family members would be expected to light the pyre. It also surprised me that there was no attempt to conceal my grandmother's blackened body as the flames consumed it, no expression of revulsion or fear among the family and friends who stood by watching and chatting.

Back at the house after the cremation, the lamas put a gold disk in the altar room. If my grandmother still hadn't left, she'd look at the disk and, not seeing her reflection, realize she was dead. In yet another ritual, a *tsampa* barley flour effigy of a female figure astride a tiger (a wrathful vehicle to dispel obstacles and speed my grandmother onward) was placed at the intersection of four roads. All of the rituals—prayers urging us to acknowledge we are dead, a severed string, a pyre lit by loved ones, a golden mirror, a tsampa effigy—made tangible the reality of letting go, helping us and my grandmother do something that seemed impossible: accept the reality of death.

Over a hot rum in the Windamere Hotel bar that evening, guests enjoying the cocktail hour in the sitting room next door, I thought about the nonattachment rituals and recalled a visit in the 1980s to the Jokhang, Tibet's holiest temple. Sacred juniper burned in a great censer by the entrance as pilgrims passed by, walking the path around the temple before proceeding inside to circumambulate the tall, jeweled statue of Jowo Rinpoche, the historical Gautama Buddha, glimmering in the smoky light of butter lamps. The scene was not much different, I'd imagined, from how it must have been sixty years earlier when my grandmother lived in Lhasa with her father and they came to the Jokhang to pray.

Following my guide, I climbed the stairs to the temple roof and we happened upon a monk working on an intricate, nearly complete sand mandala about a yard in diameter. Representing the universe and the teachings of the Buddha, the guide explained, the mandala depicted Chenrezig, Bodhisattva of Compassion, in the middle of a celestial palace. Surrounding him were deities and sacred symbols related to obstructive emotions like ignorance, hatred, and attachment, as well as positive qualities like love and joy. By contemplating a mandala, it was believed, both Buddhist practitioners and non-practitioners could enter Chenrezig's palace and engage with the teachings. Not long after the mandala was finished, the monk would sweep up the richly colored sand and pour it into a river to release the mandala's blessings for the benefit of all sentient beings.

Remembering the sand mandala that evening at the Windamere, I thought about how remarkable it was that such a magnificent work, created over weeks with painstaking intentionality and care, could vanish in a moment. But creating and then destroying a sand mandala was a ritual—both for the religious community where it was made and for members of the wider public who might witness its creation and destruction—that recognized impermanence as the nature of existence, encouraging us not to cling, to accept that one day our complex, beautiful lives will disintegrate and disappear.

I felt a deeper understanding of why the nonattachment rituals were so central to the bardo ceremonies and why my grandmother had worried about what would happen if she died while visiting us in California and couldn't have a Tibetan funeral. She believed that if you didn't let go of your old life, you "hovered about," unable to move on in bardo. The spirits of the lingering dead were said to roam Darjeeling, like the nanny with a pram who went about knocking at people's doors, disappearing the moment you said, "Who's there?" Lonely, mist-shrouded Jalapahar Cantonment was inhabited by the ghosts of British soldiers who had committed suicide. My grandmother heard from a colonel who had stayed overnight in one of the buildings that "the Scottish, with the Highland Fling, picked you up while you were sleeping and *threw* you on the ground." The story that had perhaps troubled her the most concerned a friend of hers who had been unable to let go of her husband, keeping them both tethered to their old lives: "Such a beautiful place she had, fire always lit, flowered curtains imported from England. But she was found to have gone wonky after Alfred passed off. She couldn't stop crying and that house became quite haunted. Every night, her husband would come into the parlor, sit down in his favorite chair, and read the newspaper!"

When my grandfather, Pala, died in 1980, my grandmother made extraordinary efforts to ensure that the traditional rites were carried out for him so he could move forward in bardo. They were on winter holiday in Calcutta, where, in their younger days, they had frequented the Flurys tearoom on fashionable Park Street and dined with princes and princesses, rajas and ranis, generals and ambassadors at legendary Firpo's, which had a live orchestra and a sprung dance floor. ("People used to say there's never been a dancer like your grandfather," my grandmother loved to remember. "I was always very proud to be on his arm.")

Late one night at their hotel, the December moon low over the sleeping city, my grandmother heard Pala shuffling through papers. "I'm looking for medicine, darling," he said. "I feel terrible pain in the shoulder blade."

My grandfather had suffered a heart attack, but instead of taking him to the hospital, my grandmother rushed him up to Darjeeling because she'd seen his death in a dream. "I thought, whatever will happen, let it happen in our own house," she told me. "Our home in the world where we belong, where we were born and say our prayers, where we've walked round the town greeting our friends."

In Calcutta, they knew people but had no relations. "I knew I must get your grandfather home by hook or by crook," my grandmother said. "Down there, they'd have cremated his body in the electric machine, with no prayers, nothing. We believe the soul will be hovering about the place without the prayers and the burning of the butter lamps."

Driving up from the plains "slow by slow" in mist "thick as pea soup," my grandmother brought Pala home so he could let go of the life he'd had and she could begin her journey onward without him after fifty years of marriage. ("For me there was never anyone else. And same for Pala. We never went alone anywhere, we were always together.") It didn't mean she wouldn't grieve, perhaps for a long time, but she wouldn't deepen her sorrow by clinging to what was now lost to her.

We might try to convince ourselves that we can avoid facing change until we're on our deathbeds. But not only will we ourselves one day cease to exist, throughout our lives we experience endings in ways both small (a leaf falling from a tree) and large (the loss of a loved one). Given that death, and transitions of all kinds, are inextricably intertwined with life, how can we become more accepting of change? The power of nonattachment is easy to praise but harder to put into action.

When you were young, your parents probably said that if you practiced something—piano, ballet, math—you'd get better at it. And indeed, after dedicated effort, we usually become more proficient. Studies by University of Wisconsin–Madison psychology and psychiatry professor Richard J. Davidson have shed light on how practice can help us become better at accepting change. Davidson had been researching how our minds affect our brains in ways that incline us toward negative states such as depression and anxiety when, in 1992, the Dalai Lama asked him to study whether the mind can influence the brain in ways that dispose us toward positive states. In particular, His Holiness was interested in what Davidson might discover about the brains of Tibetan monks who'd been meditating for years, developing qualities like patience and compassion.

Studying the brains of Tibetan monks and other long-term meditators, Davidson found brain activity "indicative of plasticity," which suggests that the brain can indeed be activated in new directions, even when we're adults. In a 2019 TEDxSanFrancisco talk, he explained, "Our brains are constantly changing, constantly being shaped by the forces around us." What's more, his research shows that not only do our brains have plasticity, but the ways in which they change are not necessarily beyond our control. In other words, just as you can condition your body by doing yoga or running, you can take purposeful steps to shape your brain.

Thus, we can train our brains to become more accepting of impermanence. The Dalai Lama does this by meditating every day on death. "Something which is difficult to handle, if you prepare for that, you know it," he says in the documentary *The Tibetan Book of the Dead: A Way of Life*. "Such and such is the time I will face a terrible situation, and knowing it, you prepare for it. Then when that actually happens, you've already accepted it." This kind of groundwork sounds like disaster preparedness—taking part in a tornado drill, for example—but the difference is that, while we may never be caught in a tornado, it's certain that we will experience endings in life, the final one being our own. While reflecting on endings before they occur may seem terrifying and unnecessary (Why waste the time you're alive thinking about death?), it allows us to live with less fear and die with greater equanimity. We can become at ease with change instead of trying to convince ourselves that it isn't happening or won't happen.

In "To Philosophize Is to Learn How to Die," an essay I return to often in the copy of *Essais* that I inherited from my father, Montaigne writes, "To begin depriving death of its greatest advantage over us, let us adopt a way clean contrary to that common one; let us deprive death of its strangeness; let us frequent it, let us get used to it; let us have nothing more often in mind than death."

Montaigne gives as an example the Egyptian custom of bringing in a mummified corpse during an evening of feasting and merrymaking, to remind the guests that death is an inescapable part of life. Human skull bowls and horns made from human thigh bones serve as reminders of impermanence in Tibetan tantric rituals; the presence of the deceased's body during the bardo funeral rites has a similar function. Sitting next to my grandmother's corpse in the altar room as the lamas chanted from *The Tibetan Book of the Dead* helped me feel that death was as ordinary a stage of existence as birth. It seemed in the natural order of things that just as we come into this life, we depart this life, the same way that we arrive at a party and then leave the party. Who would imagine staying forever?

In day-to-day existence, we aren't likely to drink from human skull bowls or sit next to dead bodies, but there are many ways to practice getting used to impermanence and develop a kind of muscle memory as we alter our brain's response to it. Then, when endings come, we can more easily let go of what's already lost to us. Rather than reacting with fear and denial, we can draw on the fortitude and familiarity we've developed through practice, just as we're able to run a marathon if we've trained for it.

Montaigne suggests, "Whenever a horse stumbles, a tile falls or a pin pricks however slightly, let us at once chew over this thought: 'Supposing that was death itself?'" He underscores the relationship between awareness of impermanence and liberation, observing, "To practise death is to practise freedom."

Practicing death in the everyday way Montaigne proposes can mean observing the changing light as the sun rises. On your lunch break in the park, you watch how clouds appear and morph and disappear in the sky. You observe snow melting as you walk your dog; dusk falling over the neighborhood trees and houses as you return home from work. You take note of the way everything has a beginning and an end: a meeting, a meal, a conversation, a weekend trip.

No matter how busy you are, you can spend a little time each day musing on change. Buddhist monk Matthieu Ricard, known as "the happiest person in the world," says that before he became a monk, he began training his mind through brief daily reflection: "The fact is, it is possible to undergo serious spiritual training by devoting some time every day to meditation. More people than you might think do so, while leading regular family lives and doing absorbing work.... When I was [studying cellular genetics] at the Institut Pasteur and immersed in Parisian life, the few moments I reserved every day for contemplation brought me enormous benefits."

You might reflect on who you are now versus who you were as a child, a goal or belief system you've outgrown, a lifestyle you once enjoyed. You can meditate on time seen in terms of mountain ranges and lakes and forests that appeared hundreds of millions of years ago, what writer John McPhee calls "deep time." Becoming familiar with deep time while writing *Annals of the Former World*, McPhee told me in a conversation for my bardo interview series, opened his eyes to "what a million years is versus our lifetime," and led him to be more accepting of impermanence. He's received letters from cancer patients who say that thinking about deep time has made it easier for them to let go of the life they had before falling ill.

Sometimes I contemplate change by thinking about my grandmother's house in Darjeeling and seeing her tiny body being carried out the front door for the journey to the cremation ground. I go through the dim, silent rooms and look at the things she loved: the silver tea service she used when entertaining her father's guests in the early 1900s, the satin high-heeled shoes she wore to galas at the Gymkhana Club, when she was known as the belle of Darjeeling and her dance card was always full. I study the *thangka* scroll paintings depicting the life of the Buddha: his birth in the garden of Lumbini, his enlightenment under a bodhi tree, his death in a forest grove.

*The Tibetan Book of the Dead* suggests that meditating on our "tutelary deity" can help us accept the truth of our situation. In a footnote, Evans-Wentz explains, "The favourite deity of the deceased is the tutelary...usually one of the Buddhas or Bodhisattvas." Maybe yours is the Buddha or the Dalai Lama; a teacher, your partner, a friend, an ancestor; Jane Austen or Michael Jordan or Bono. If you're resisting change in your marriage or your job, you might ask yourself: *Would the Buddha remain in this marriage? Would Jane Austen stay in this job?*

I like to think about Julia Child, who had a very Buddhist outlook. In *My Life in France*, she writes about leaving La Pitchoune, the cottage in the Provençal village of Plascassier where she and her husband, Paul, spent their winters and springs for almost thirty years. Elderly and infirm, Paul could no longer make the journey from the United States, and their friends had begun "to slip off into the Great Blue Yonder." Child says, "Without Paul to share the house with, or...all of our other favorite friends and family, it had come time to relinquish La Pitchoune." She continues, "I've always felt that when I'm done with something I just walk away from it—*fin!*" And, "Now I was moving forward again, into new experiences, in new places, with new people."

By practicing impermanence, we can begin to free ourselves from dread of change and feel greater happiness. Gradually conditioning our brains to be more comfortable with the transitory nature of life changes the way that we engage with it. Even as we experience emotions such as fear or sadness, we can ease our hearts by coming from a place of acceptance rather than attachment or denial, just like my grandmother did when my grandfather was dying. We can recognize that, as the Buddha taught, it's the belief that we (and everything around us) are solid and unchanging that most makes us suffer, rather than the ephemerality of life.

Living in Japan offers many lessons in nonattachment. I was struck by this when I returned to Tokyo after Mac died and went to pick up his ashes, not something I'd considered doing until the veterinarian called and said he had them ready for us.

The vet told me that his collie had recently passed away and he kept the ashes on his mantel.

"Really?" I thought he was joking.

"Every day, I bow to them and say good morning!"

At home, I opened the silver and white brocade cover on the porcelain urn and peered inside. There were bones rather than ashes: Mac's jawbone, with the eye socket, was almost intact. It didn't seem right to scatter bones, so I decided that we'd bury them. But instead, I found myself setting the urn on our *tansu* chest in the living room, and that's where it has stayed. I feel more at peace with losing Mac when I look at the beautiful cover with his name written on it in katakana, マック, and the date of his death, 2022.6.3. He was born in Shizuoka Prefecture, near the ocean and Mount Fuji. When the time comes for us to return to America, we'll leave his bones there. For now, his presence in our house is a way to practice death, a reminder of the wisdom of accepting impermanence.

Awareness of the fleeting nature of existence is a fundamental part of life in Japanese culture. Even the most joyful moments—falling in love, giving birth—are infused with the sorrow of knowing they will end. In an ode to brief splendor, the *sakura* cherry blossoms in spring are cherished for the beauty of the lush pink flowers, the promise of their disappearance integral to their loveliness. People eat and drink and sing under the blossoms, conscious that in only a few short days, the petals will begin to swirl in the air like fragrant, ethereal snow. Acknowledgment, rather than denial, of impermanence is vital to the experience.

Japanese expressions that relate to this recognition are never far from my mind: *mono no aware*, the contemplative melancholy that arises in the presence of ephemeral beauty, as when viewing cherry blossoms; *wabi-sabi*, the wistful appreciation of aging, decay, and imperfection (seen, for example, in the scarred wooden floor of the house I've lived in and loved for years); and *mujō*, impermanence, evoked in these famous lines at the beginning of the thirteenth-century samurai epic *Tale of the Heike*: "The sound of the Gion Shōja bells echoes the impermanence of all things; the color of the *śāla* flowers reveals the truth that the prosperous must decline. The proud do not endure, they are like a dream on a spring night; the mighty fall at last, they are as dust before the wind."

Transitoriness is woven into the atmosphere in Tokyo, where I've lived for over three decades now. In fall and winter, the *yaki-imo* sweet potato vendor winds through our neighborhood, his elegiac song—*Roasted sweet potatoes! Stone-roasted sweet potatoes!*—floating on the cold twilight air. Walking around is like being in a dream where the world you know has vanished: mazelike alleyways, streets without names, houses that all have the same address. The cityscape is shifting, Escheresque, a jumble of architectural styles ranging from traditional tile-roofed residences to futuristic skyscrapers. Stairs, rooms, verandas, are tacked on any which way; a friend looking to rent a place was shown one that, on the second floor, had a door that once led to somewhere but now opened onto empty space. Homes are seen as temporary dwellings, built to last only twenty or thirty years and then be demolished. At the same time, because of the aging population and the falling birthrate, steep taxes, and the hope that long-gone children will return and take over the property, houses stand vacant, even in centrally located areas. You see these ghostly *akiya* everywhere: overgrown with ivy, metal shutters pulled down over the windows.

Things in Tokyo—as in many other modern cities—are constantly changing. I arrange to meet someone at one of my favorite cafés, but when we arrive, it's gone. A 7/11 becomes a parking lot, a gyoza restaurant turns into a reflexology salon, a *sentō* public bathhouse is replaced by an eyewear shop. Pachinko parlors, love hotels, and dog clothing boutiques materialize next to temples and rock gardens. The juxtaposition of the new and the traditional makes the city seem like a palimpsest, contemporary stories overlying old ones. Temples and shrines are among the few things you can count on, though shrines like ancient Ise Jingu southeast of Kyoto are torn down every twenty years and rebuilt, reflecting the cycle of life and death and—as the tradition endures—the unchanging truth and beauty of impermanence.

Whether you live in Tokyo or some other large city, in the mountains or by the sea, the world around us offers ample opportunity to practice death. In the midst of our everyday lives, we can train our brains to accept change by taking note of it in the fluid urban landscape, the changing seasons, the weathering of a porch rail, the dramatic new formation of a beach after a storm.

Struggling against transformation and endings is like raging against the setting sun. The more we cling—to a place we once lived, a relationship, a way of thinking, a loved one who is gone—the more pain we feel. But what it means to embrace impermanence can seem complicated. Should you recommit to or leave your marriage, work harder at or quit your job, rekindle or break off a friendship?

The more accepting we are of change, the less our vision is obscured by illusion, allowing us to better see what choice or path forward is right for us. Developing this perspective may not seem especially urgent, but resistance to change can undermine our physical, emotional, and spiritual well-being. One of the most striking aspects of denial is that we're attached to something that no longer exists—a fulfilling marriage, your mother when she was young—however much we may wish it did. Instinctively, we hold on, but in so doing, we work against the happiness we seek. There are endings we can do something about (a job that's no longer right for us) and ones we can't (the death of a parent), but whatever the case, we'll suffer less if we acknowledge what is.

As Evans-Wentz writes in his introduction to *The Tibetan Book of the Dead*, "The whole aim of the *Bardo Thödol* teaching... is to cause the Dreamer to awaken into Reality." Just as the deceased can progress on her bardo journey by admitting she is dead, we can move forward in life by facing our reality.

# 4.
# PLAY, ENGAGE, STOP AND PAY ATTENTION

Attention is living; inattention is dying. The attentive never stop; the inattentive are dead already.

—The Buddha, *Dhammapada*, 21

The unfortunate thing is to have wasted such a large portion of the chance you had to live a richer life.... Never stopped but were distracted by noise, expectations and images, instead of dwelling on what you were doing at this moment and what you might do differently. I don't mean to say that any of this is easy, but it may be worthwhile.

—Erling Kagge
*Silence: In the Age of Noise*

When my grandmother died, the lamas sat next to her body day and night. If one lama took a break, another came so she was never alone. In the morning, sunlight spilled through the lacy curtains and illuminated the statues of the buddhas and Guru Rinpoche. At night, the moon rose over Kanchenjunga and the Tibetan Plateau.

Together with my mother and our relations, I listened in the altar room to the lamas as they chanted from *The Tibetan Book of the Dead*. Again and again, they urged my grandmother to pay attention:

> Let not thy mind be distracted.
> Thou wilt pay undistracted attention to that
>   with which I am about to set thee face to face.
> O nobly-born, listen undistractedly.

The room itself felt like an embodiment of focused attention. On the altar were my grandmother's prayer book and beads, butter lamps and silver offering bowls. Every day for more than half a century, the altar had been dusted, the butter lamps and incense lit, and fresh water poured into the offering bowls. My grandmother had begun and ended each day here, saying, "I bow down to all the lamas, bow down to all the buddhas, bow down to all the manuscripts." This was where she said the traditional prayers passed down over the centuries, the same ones she'd said with her father in their altar room in Tibet; at the great Lhasa monasteries of Drepung and Sera; at the Jokhang Temple. "When my father and I stood before Jowo Rinpoche at the Jokhang and prayed," my grandmother told me, "right away I felt something different, like my mind became very peaceful and I could see now this is this, that is that."

Having grown up without religion, I had little interest in prayer when I first began visiting my grandmother after college. She liked to tell me that prayer was essential to seeing that happiness is available to everyone; I suspected she sensed the discontent that had led me to Darjeeling, and I knew that "everyone" included me.

"The old Tibetan ladies at the Jokhang prayed *om mani padme hum* with their prayer beads thousands and thousands of times from morning to night," my grandmother said. "In Darjeeling, we count one or two hundred, we haven't got time to count thousands." For me as a modern American girl, she added with a fond smile, "perhaps ten or twenty" would be enough. I wasn't sure what form prayer could take in my case, but through the time I spent with my grandmother over the years and what I've learned about Buddhism, I've come to see it in terms of attention. As French philosopher Simone Weil said, "Attention, taken to its highest degree, is the same thing as prayer."

# *PLAY, ENGAGE, STOP AND PAY ATTENTION*

*The Tibetan Book of the Dead* urges the dead to pay attention as they are set face to face with reality. If they're inattentive to the lamas' prayers and instructions, they float along in the dark, "wandering in [*samsara* suffering]," diverted from the path to liberation.

In the bardo of life, we may drift through the months and years, immersed in thoughts and reveries, and this becomes our comfort zone. What our distracted minds perceive turns into our reality, and we may have the uneasy feeling that we're dwelling in a strange parallel universe, able to sense our real lives but not to live them. According to "A Wandering Mind Is an Unhappy Mind," a 2010 study by Harvard psychologists Matthew Killingsworth and Daniel Gilbert published in *Science*, we spend almost half our waking hours consumed by thoughts and daydreams, and this leaves us dissatisfied. "Unlike other animals, human beings spend a lot of time thinking about what is not going on around them," they explain, "contemplating events that happened in the past, might happen in the future, or will never happen at all." (This echoes something Montaigne is believed to have said: "My life has been full of terrible misfortunes, most of which never happened.")

Preoccupied and restless, we worry that something is missing, or that we're missing out on something, and we wonder if we'll ever find contentment. Driven by amorphous, insatiable desire, we search. Like the dead as they journey through bardo, we may find ourselves adrift in the realm of *preta* hungry ghosts, a world populated by wretched beings with throats as thin as a piece of hair and stomachs as big as the Grand Canyon—"Never enough eats or drinks for them," my grandmother used to say.

In the preta world, *The Tibetan Book of the Dead* tells us, there are "desolate treeless plains and shallow caverns, jungle glades and forest wastes.... If one goeth there,... one will suffer various pangs of hunger and thirst." This quenchless desire is known as *tanhā* (craving), which the *Merriam-Webster Dictionary* defines as "an intense desire for life."

I first became familiar with hungry ghosts in my childhood, when I'd perch on the living room sofa and study a *thangka* scroll painting that my mother had brought with her to America. The painting showed fierce, buffalo-headed Yama, Lord of Death and symbol of impermanence, holding the Wheel of Life in his clawlike hands and feet. The Wheel contained illustrations of the realms in which we can be reborn as we go around and around in samsara suffering: god, demigod, human, animal, hell, and—the one I especially hoped to avoid—hungry ghost, where skeletal beings with distended bellies kneeled in supplication as flames consumed them.

## PLAY, ENGAGE, STOP AND PAY ATTENTION

    Years later, I would remember those hideous creatures when I came upon a parable from the *Lotus Sutra* in which a man's children are playing inside a broken-down house that catches fire. In the house,

> Foxes, wolves, and jackals
> Bit and trampled each other,
> Ripping apart the bodies of the dead,
> Scattering bone and tissue.
> Following them came packs of dogs
> That fought with each other, snatching, and
>     grabbing.
> Gaunt with hunger, they skulked about,
> Roving in search of food,
> Fighting and scuffling,
> Snarling and growling.
> Such were the terrifying and degraded
>     conditions
> Into which that house had fallen....
> [The] house
> Suddenly caught fire
> On all four sides at once.
> As the flames reached full blaze,
> Ridgepoles, rafters, beams, and pillars
> Trembled, split, snapped, and broke apart,
> Falling with explosive sounds.
> Walls and partitions crumbled.

The man urges his children to leave the house, telling them,

> The sufferings here are already hard to deal
>   with,
> How much more so in the midst of this raging
>   fire.

But lost in their play, too distracted to notice the flames, the children pay no attention to their father.

In life, we are the children and the father is the Buddha. The house is the world of samsara, the cycle of death and rebirth. We go around and around in this cycle, trapped in aggression and fear and delusion. It's possible to exit the burning house and live an enlightened existence, free of suffering, the parable tells us, but to do so, we must stop playing our games. In other words, we must give up our distractions.

The Buddha persuades the children to leave the house by offering them "rare toys" in the form of beautiful carts. The children rush outside and they're each presented with an ox-drawn cart, "magnificently adorned and splendidly decorated," which symbolizes the Buddha's teachings. "Ecstatic with joy," they ride about "just as they wished, without hindrance."

"Distraction" is from the Latin *distractionem*, which means "a pulling apart, separating," and *distrahere*, "to draw in different directions." Like a Harry Potterish incantation—*Distractionem distrahere!*—distraction bewitches us and makes it hard to see what's happening right before our eyes. ("Your brain needs glasses!" my son, Henry, said one day when I was only half-listening as I made dinner.) We may become so distracted that it's as if we're living in a bubble; so certain of our environment that we feel there's no need to observe it.

In Buddhism, distraction is known as "monkey mind." Our minds monkey around, chattering and screeching, swinging from vines and leaping from tree to tree. Did you hurt a friend's feelings, could you be a better son or daughter, what if you don't have enough money to retire, will you get dementia like your father, is climate change going to make the planet unlivable for us all? Paradoxically, this distractedness makes us feel that we're paying attention to the important things in life when, in fact, it keeps us from focusing on what really matters. We end up obsessing over hypotheticals instead of engaging with reality.

The way we organize our days can also distract us. The modern glorification of productivity makes it seem like we should be doing as many things as possible as quickly as possible. Accomplishing a lot provides a fleeting hungry-ghost satisfaction that often transforms into a feeling of being disconnected from the beating heart of your life. At the end of a "productive" day, you feel like you've eaten a bag of potato chips instead of a nourishing meal, depleted by the combination of extreme busyness and failure to devote time to the things you care about the most. In *The Tibetan Book of Living and Dying*, a guide based on *The Tibetan Book of the Dead*, lama and teacher Sogyal Rinpoche remarks on this phenomenon: "If we look into our lives, we will see clearly how many unimportant tasks, so-called 'responsibilities,' accumulate to fill them up. One master compares them to 'housekeeping in a dream.' We tell ourselves we want to spend time on the important things of life, but there never *is* any time. Even simply to get up in the morning, there is so much to do: open the window, make the bed, take a shower, brush your teeth, feed the dog or cat... the list is endless."

Sometimes we do notice things but only pay vague attention to them, with potentially catastrophic results. Perhaps you're dimly aware that the hill behind your house is eroding with each passing season, exposing the roots of the tall tree at the top; one day, the tree falls on your roof. At work, you've been somewhat conscious over the past months of being given unimportant tasks and excluded from strategic meetings, but you just keep doing what you're doing and are astonished when your boss asks you to leave. As a parent, you sense that your happy-go-lucky child is growing withdrawn and moody; absorbed in the daily practicalities of caring for the family, you're stunned when the school counselor says your child needs therapy. Sometimes, inattention can adversely affect our physical health: In college, I was aware of overwhelming fatigue and an increasingly yellowish tint to my skin, but, swamped with assignments, I didn't pay attention to the clues that something was wrong. Finally, a near-collapse forced me to see a doctor, who diagnosed me with severe anemia.

There's a powerful example of the dangers of inattention in Amy Tan's novel *The Joy Luck Club*, a story about four Chinese mothers and their American daughters. One of the daughters, Rose, is shocked when her husband, Ted, tells her he wants a divorce. She has always left it to him to decide things for them (where to go on holiday, when to start a family), focusing only on her graphic design work. "[I ignored] the world around me," she says, "obsessing only over what was in front of me: my T-square, my X-acto knife, my blue pencil." Things change when Ted, a dermatologist, loses a malpractice lawsuit and no longer wants to shoulder all the responsibility in their marriage. He insists that Rose start making decisions as well, but she continues to defer to him, even as she's aware on some level of Ted's growing unhappiness. Only when Ted says he wants to end the marriage does she finally pay attention to the gulf that has opened between them, saying, "I think about my marriage, how I had seen the signs, really I had. But I just let it happen."

Failures of attention can blind us to reality not only in our personal sphere but also in the sphere of society, when we're inattentive to the ethical dimensions of life. In his Baccalaureate Address to the Princeton Class of 2023, New York University philosophy and law professor Kwame Anthony Appiah said, "It seems to me increasingly that an ethical life can almost be defined in terms of habits of attention.... When you don't *see* poor people, when you don't *see* refugees, when you don't *see* abuse, when you don't *see* discrimination, what's happening can be described, morally, as an attention deficit." He added, "It isn't only that injustice can arise from inattention; inattention can itself be a form of injustice."

Inattention as a form of injustice can be understood in terms of the Buddhist belief that every person, regardless of social and economic circumstances, seeks and deserves happiness. As the Dalai Lama says, "We are all the same as human beings. We are born the same way, we die the same way, and we all want to lead happy lives." When our foundational perspective in life (intentional or not) ignores this, we deny other people their humanity. What's more, although not paying attention to our societal sphere can seem necessary given that we have limited time and energy, it can lead us to denial of our own humanity, to feelings of isolation and meaninglessness, that sense of being cut off from real life.

## PLAY, ENGAGE, STOP AND PAY ATTENTION

*The Tibetan Book of the Dead* counsels us to pay attention, but when I was young I felt it was better to be distracted. A child of divorce, I had an emotionally chaotic home life, and I learned to remove myself mentally while remaining physically present. I became adept at mind wandering to beautiful, serene places I'd seen on TV or in magazines: a room in Paris, the balcony doors open to a balmy spring evening; a twilit room in old Tangier. The places I imagined were always rooms, spaces with a door I could close to shut everything out. Think for a moment about where your mind goes when it wanders: Does this reflect something about your life?

Distraction helped me survive when I was a girl, but I carried it with me into adulthood, where—like a vestigial pair of wings—it served me less well. Used to zoning out, I'd lose the thread of the conversation at dinner with friends. I'd give an irrelevant answer during an interview because I hadn't listened to the question. I'd make a mistake on a work assignment because I hadn't paid attention to the instructions.

This changed when I arrived in Tokyo after six months in Darjeeling, planning to make money teaching English so I could go on to start my life in Paris. I expected a teeming neon metropolis, but instead stumbled upon the tranquil room of my own that I'd dreamed of for so long. Through a notice on a grocery store bulletin board, I found a wooden teahouse that was a *yo-jo-han*, one room of about eighty square feet, in the northwest part of the city. It had been built for the grandmother behind the main residence, and I thought perhaps she'd been a tea ceremony master, teaching the traditional art to people in the neighborhood. After she died, the family started renting out the place; they offered it to me for 35,000 yen (about $150) a month, and I eagerly accepted.

The teahouse had a *tatami* straw mat floor, *fusuma* paper-covered doors painted with delicate flowers, a cold-water metal sink, a two-burner gas stove with a grill, and a toilet (there was no shower, so I used the nearby public bathhouse). On the floor in a corner of the room sat a big black rotary phone that never rang because I didn't know anyone. A *tokonoma* alcove held a scroll painting of stylized *kanji* characters, with space in front for a ceramic bowl or a vase with a sprig of cherry blossoms. Paper-paneled *shōji* doors slid open onto a narrow veranda overlooking a tiny garden with leafy bamboo, wisteria, and a plum tree that burst into fragrant white bloom in spring.

With thin walls and no insulation, my teahouse was open to the elements, which encouraged me to pay attention to my environment. I listened to cicadas shrill in the summer heat and snow slip from the tile roof on frosty evenings. Japanese onomatopoeia gave me a new awareness of rain: *shito-shito ame*, a drizzly, quiet rain; *shobo-shobo ame*, also a drizzly, quiet rain but in a somewhat negative sense; *potsu-potsu*, small raindrops, and *bota-bota*, fat raindrops, hitting the ground when it started to rain; *para-para*, the patter of rain on the window; and *zaa-zaa*, a heavy downpour. *Kigo* season words heightened my consciousness of the natural world around me: *shunshū*, spring sadness; *aoarashi*, a breeze blowing through the lush green leaves of summer; *aki no koe*, the voice of autumn, like the song of the bell cricket; *fuyugomori*, winter solitude.

Smelling the straw of the tatami, watching the light change through the shoji, I reveled in the peace and seclusion. In the evenings, I lay on my futon gazing at the silhouette of a cat that perched, sphinxlike, on the old stone wall outside, the silence broken only by occasional footsteps in the alley. I read Yasunari Kawabata's *Snow Country*, about an ill-starred love affair between a married man and a geisha; *In Praise of Shadows*, Jun'ichirō Tanizaki's essay on Japanese concepts of beauty; and *The Pillow Book*, a diary written in the tenth and eleventh centuries by court lady Sei Shōnagon. I loved Shōnagon's attention to the details of everyday life, as seen, for example, in the entry "Things That Give a Clean Feeling":

> An earthen cup. A new metal bowl.
> A rush mat.

> The play of the light on water as one pours it
> into a vessel.
>
> A new wooden chest.

I read *Narrow Road to the Interior*, a prose and haiku narrative by seventeenth-century pilgrim-poet Matsuo Bashō, and imagined that my teahouse resembled the rustic thatched-roof hut Bashō had lived in by the Sumida River in eastern Tokyo. He was said to have written one of his most famous haiku there, a poem about the eternal and the now that I liked to think about as I looked out at the garden:

> At the ancient pond
> a frog plunges into
> the sound of water

With the passing weeks and months, I grew increasingly attuned to my environment and was surprised to feel years of repressed sorrow begin to surge forth like a hidden tide breaking through to the surface. To my greater surprise, this came as a relief. Alone in the room I'd despaired of ever finding, I could at last pay attention to the anguish I'd distracted myself from for so long: the alienation I'd felt growing up and grief over my parents' divorce.

As the world without and within came into focus, the precision of my larger surroundings deepened my sense of being able to see more clearly. Though a densely populated city of about twelve million, Tokyo consisted mostly of tidy neighborhoods, each with a mom-and-pop grocery store, tatami maker, flower shop, bakery, tofu shop, post office, bank, and little park. In the mornings, shopkeepers hosed the pavement in front of their stores and greeted children walking to school; housewives hung freshly laundered clothing out to dry.

The harmony of life in Tokyo extended to personal safety as well. People didn't lock their doors, and, astonishingly, women could walk alone at any hour. I realized how fractured my attention had been, not only by the emotional danger I'd grown up with but also by the physical danger that came with being female in America. Girls I knew had been raped and a close childhood friend was murdered. When I was young, I would tiptoe around the house at night, checking and double-checking that the doors and windows were secured; I searched my closet before going to bed to make sure no one was hiding there. For years, I dreamed that someone was trying to break in and, frantic, I was dialing the police again and again, unable to get through.

I traveled alone in Europe, Latin America, and India, wanting to feel free, but I couldn't shake my fear. I would barricade myself in my hotel rooms at night by pushing furniture against the door and I rarely talked with strangers, especially men. On high alert, I scanned my environment like a soldier assessing enemy territory.

In Tokyo, I felt safe, at home in the world for the first time. Walking down the street, I looked around rather than keeping my gaze fixed straight ahead, and I didn't have to detour around construction sites to avoid wolf whistles and vulgar comments. I roamed wherever and whenever I pleased, exploring shrines and gyoza joints and fish markets; I meandered about the city, open to whatever the moment might bring. I lingered in coffee houses and jazz bars, observing and reflecting on my surroundings, a flâneuse instead of a fighter.

~

The mind is like a team of horses that, given the chance, will charge off in different directions (hence, distraction is "a pulling apart, separating"). The challenge is to take hold of the reins. *The Tibetan Book of the Dead* tells us that the mind can be guided "like the controlling of a horse's mouth by means of a bridle." Evans-Wentz explains in a footnote: "As with a bridle, controlling the bit and the course of the horse, so with this Doctrine the deceased can be directed or turned in his after-death progression."

The Buddhist texts tell us that around 500 BCE, Prince Siddhartha Gautama became the Buddha by leaving his father's palace and turning his mind toward awakening. Late one evening in the North Indian capital of Kapilavastu,

Gautama shed his fine clothing and ornaments for a simple yellow robe and walked away from the sleeping city, stars wheeling in the blue-black sky, the smell of earth and rain in his nostrils. His father, the king, had tried to shield him from the realities of the world, but on excursions into town, Gautama had seen an old man, a sick man, a dead body, and a wandering monk. Having witnessed old age, illness, and death—and inspired by the monk's example—he wished to unshackle himself from the distractions of the palace and find a way to end the suffering we all endure. After traveling the Gangetic Plain for six years, he reached enlightenment and became the Buddha.

Of course, much as we may desire to turn our minds in a new direction, most of us can't, or prefer not to, walk away from our present existence. How, then, can we alter our habits of attention within the rhythms and responsibilities of day-to-day life?

I discovered one way of doing this when, after a year in Tokyo, I moved to Chicago to work and apply to graduate school. I enrolled in an evening writing course and would arrive preoccupied and tired after a long day at the office; the other students appeared to be in a similar state. The teacher started the class by saying, "Let your listening go out the window." We'd fall silent and I'd feel my attention shift into the present moment—almost a physical sensation—as I listened to music from a passing car, people talking in the street, the flight calls of geese over Lake Michigan, the rumble of distant thunder.

I've continued this practice for many years now. I close my eyes and listen to the sounds around me as I commute on the train or wait in line at the grocery store. If you close your eyes and listen for a few moments, then switch back and forth between thoughts and listening, thoughts and listening, you'll see how listening brings you into alignment with the moment. Sometimes I'll sit for a while—on a park bench, in a café, by the kitchen window—and listen to the singsong voices of girls skipping rope, the clink of coffee cups, the *shush-shush* of a neighbor sweeping leaves. Little by little, day after day, practices like this change our attention to the world around us.

In Tokyo, I used to go every week to a neighborhood temple that allowed foreigners to take part in *zazen*, or Japanese seated meditation. Toward the end of each session, the priest would give a talk. Sometimes this was about embracing "beginner's mind" and not-knowing; how coming from a place of curiosity changes the way we pay attention, opening us to the present moment. This made me think of Montaigne's famous motto, "Que sais-je?" (*What do I know?*), his belief that a spirit of inquiry keeps us from falling into complacency and not noticing the world we live in. Montaigne brought this spirit to life in his essays, paying minute attention to things like sadness, the education of children, sleep, and imagination.

I would also think of my father, a man of endless curiosity. Whenever I visited him at his apartment in San Francisco, he'd ask about my friends and school life; introduce me to music, such as the *alegrías flamenco* that originated in Cadiz, the province in Andalusia where I was born; explain scientific facts that intrigued him (if you combined a quart of water with a quart of alcohol, you lost about 10 percent of the volume because of the way the molecules fit together); recall natural phenomena that he found unforgettably lovely, like the thousands of fireflies he'd seen blinking in synchrony one night in India. He was always completely present, listening and speaking with careful attention.

When Henry was a small boy, he taught me a memorable lesson in not-knowing and being in the moment. We'd just arrived in Boston from Tokyo, and he was wide awake at 3 a.m. because of jet lag. It was winter and raining, and as we lay together on the sofa, my thoughts wandered to how nice it would be to get back to sleep, what I had to do that day, whether I'd forgotten to pack anything. Next to me, Henry was quiet, listening. "Where does the rain come from?" he asked. My focus shifted and I heard the rain thrumming on the rooftop, felt the weight of my son's little body on my arm, noticed the headlights of a passing car arc across the ceiling.

Now that my children are grown, it's my mini schnauzer, Beau, who reminds me to pay attention. On our walks,

I watch as he investigates things I might not otherwise take note of: a fan-shaped gingko leaf swirling in the wind, a pair of stone foxes guarding a tiny shrine at the end of an alley. In *On Looking: A Walker's Guide to the Art of Observation*, Barnard professor and dog cognition researcher Alexandra Horowitz writes about having a similar kind of experience with her dog when they go for a walk in her Manhattan neighborhood. As he sniffs about, she observes "things on our route I had never noticed before: small faucets attached to sides of buildings; brass pegs in the sidewalk that are, I subsequently learned, part of a national registry of such pegs; the difference in the ratio of shade to sun on the north and south sides of the street." Following your dog's lead, a routine outing can change into an in-the-moment engagement with the world around you.

Another way of seizing the reins and changing how we pay attention is related to what's known in Tibetan as *kora*, which means to circumambulate a place without any goal of arrival or reward. In the West, "going around in circles" usually refers to wasting time or acting in vain, but in the Tibetan way of looking at it, walking in circles brings us deeper and deeper into the moment and ourselves. Kora can be performed by circumambulating a natural site, such as a mountain or a lake; an object or a place created by humans, like a stupa, a monastery, or a hamlet; or the residence of a spiritual master. Famous Tibetan sites include the Jokhang Temple in Tibet and the Dalai Lama's compound in Dharamsala, India. Kora may also be carried out along straight paths or roads, especially in urban areas.

In 1965, Beat poets Gary Snyder, Allen Ginsberg, and Philip Whalen circumambulated Mount Tamalpais (Tam), a peak near where I grew up in the San Francisco Bay Area. Tam is often compared to holy mountains in India and Tibet: There are clear streams and verdant meadows; the sun glints on the Pacific and hawks glide in the sky. Snyder, Ginsberg, and Whalen "opened the mountain," blowing a conch shell as they commenced the walk. The idea had come to Snyder and Ginsberg during their travels in Asia, where they learned about the ritual circumambulation of sacred Mount Kailash in western Tibet.

As Snyder, Ginsberg, and Whalen walked around Tam, they paused at creeks, rock outcroppings, caves, and redwood groves to bow and chant mantras, establishing a tradition that continues on the mountain today. "The main thing," Snyder said in an interview with UC Davis English professor David Robertson, "is to pay your regards, to play, to engage, to stop and pay attention. It's just a way of stopping and looking—at your self too." Whalen had similar feelings: "At that time [circumambulating Tam] stopped me from worrying a lot," he said in the same interview. Short on money, having just lost his father, and about to leave San Francisco for Japan in the hope of a better life, he was "worrying about a whole lot of things right then." But he found that he "didn't have to worry as long as I was busy walking around the mountain.... I was able just to open up to things and see them."

We can perform our own ritual walks in places that have personal meaning to us. For me, these include Ghoom Monastery in Darjeeling; Montparnasse Cemetery in Paris, the final resting place of one of my literary heroes, Marguerite Duras; and the Tokyo neighborhood where I lived in the teahouse all those years ago. For you, it might be a local pond, a church, the town where you lived as a child. No matter what the route, kora holds the possibility of shifting the way we pay attention. It creates time and space for a fertile kind of mind wandering, the birth of new perspectives as we focus our attention on our immediate surroundings, not distracted by hungry ghost desires and worries.

∼

About fifteen years ago, I learned something new about paying attention when I visited Bhutia Busty Monastery in Darjeeling one misty morning. Passing through a gate painted with undulating snakes like the serpent gods said to guard *terma* treasure texts (some of which were hidden in monasteries), I approached the two-story maroon-and-white building. As I stepped across the threshold, a lama introduced himself and offered to show me around.

On the first floor, I admired murals of Buddhist deities, and we then proceeded upstairs, where there was a large statue of Guru Rinpoche. The statue wore a lotus-shaped hat adorned with turquoise and coral. The eyebrows swooped down to the bridge of the nose, and heavy pendants hung from the ears. According to legend, the monastery housed the original manuscript of Guru Rinpoche's *Bardo Thödol*. I asked the lama if they owned such a manuscript, and if so, whether I could have a look.

"People often inquire to me: 'Please, can we see *The Tibetan Book of the Dead*?'" he replied. "But we never take it out."

Instead, he taught the bardo principles himself to foreigners who came to the monastery to study Buddhism. "It's my passion," he explained. If I wished, I could be in touch with him about the teachings by cell phone and email. "Some say better I spend more time studying, praying, but"—he spread his hands wide—"who knows your mind? You can never say this person or that person is not doing his practice. Now I'm talking with you, but I'm still with my practice."

Reflecting on our conversation as I walked back through town to my grandmother's house, I realized that the lama had taught me something important about the bardo principle of nondistraction. For him, being with his practice meant knowing that teaching—even though it takes time away from study and prayer—isn't a distraction because it's aligned with his values as a lama. I saw that the alignment between action and values can help us to live with less distraction and more awareness, to guide the horse (our mind) with a bridle, rather than desperately clinging to its neck as the beast thunders along.

To expand on this idea, aligning our actions with what's important to us (seizing the reins) by making sure we're devoting time to what we care about helps us to be attentive and present in all spheres of our life. Perhaps this means journaling for a few minutes every evening, learning a new language, or taking piano lessons. You might do more with your partner, volunteer in your community, or start a humanitarian project. In this way, we can avoid falling prey to the distraction of deferred or unfulfilled dreams, however small or large, running like a background program in our minds as we go about our days.

It's often said that we can become more attentive by shifting the balance between everyday tasks and what we care most about. In other words, spend less time on the mundane and more time on what's important. But the quality of our attention depends less on what we're doing than on our frame of mind while we're doing it; knowing that our priorities are in order allows us to spend more time in a state of awareness, no matter what we're engaged in. This helps you to be present when you're cooking and cleaning and taking your child to the dentist—instead of fretting about what you'd rather be doing, you can relax into the moment. You can be like Montaigne, who said, "When I dance, I dance. When I sleep, I sleep."

As conscious attention becomes our way of being in the world, we undergo a profound shift in our experience of life. Instead of feeling like we're moving (rushing) from hour to hour, day to day—our attention fractured as we try in vain to catch up with all that we want to do and must do, wondering if we're just hamsters in the wheel—we can be more aware in each moment, and gradually that becomes our comfort zone.

~

When we get used to being more present, we gain a clearer view of the relationship between attention and interdependence. I experienced this when I moved to Tokyo, where, as I became less distracted, I grew more aware of the ways in which we're interconnected.

In Japan, interdependence is seen in your relationship to the natural world. We should live in harmony with nature rather than trying to control it: When I bought an air conditioner during the sweltering Tokyo summer, my neighbor said, "But it's summer!" Many Japanese, both old and young, use handheld and electric fans. They prefer a deep-mind cooling arrived at through the refreshing, lyrical ring of a glass wind bell with a poem tied to the clapper;

the view of a garden through a bamboo blind; the reflection of clouds in a stone water basin; the ripple of a *noren* door curtain.

This outlook is rooted in the indigenous Shinto religion, where humans and nature are believed to coexist in a web of interdependence. It can be seen in architectural design that embraces flow between interior space and the surrounding environment; in rituals like the tea ceremony, *sadō* (the way of tea), where the flowers, wall scrolls, and bowls that are used vary according to the season. It's the relationship with nature that I sensed when I lived in the teahouse, which felt like an element of the natural world rather than protection against it.

In Japanese society, mutuality with people is also emphasized, where what you do is not so much about personal achievement as about the good of all. The first-person plural imperative is frequently used—*Ganbarō! Ki o tsukemashō!* (Let's do our best! Let's be careful!)—and the pronoun for "I" is often omitted from sentences. One should avoid being *wagamama* (selfish, egotistical, self-indulgent) and take care not to *meiwaku o kakeru* (cause trouble to others). A student of mine who'd returned from a homestay in the United States told me that she found America to be a "dreamy" country: "Everybody wants to only realize their own dream," she said, "not thinking about the other people." In Japan, I'm often thanked for my cooperation—*Go kyōryoku arigatō gozaimasu*—before I've decided whether I'm going to do whatever I'm being asked to do. At first, I felt resistance to this as an individualistic American and from what I knew my psychiatrist father would say: If someone thanked you for your cooperation before you agreed to their request, they were trying to legislate your behavior. But I've come to understand this custom as a marker of community, a way of saying we're all in this together.

My awareness of interdependence has been heightened by what I've learned from the Buddhist teachings, which tell us that paying attention to our connection to others is part of the framework of belonging, a perspective that orients us toward empathy and participation as we journey together through life with everyone else on the planet.

In a conversation with me for my interview series about bardo, author Andrew Sean Greer discussed attention as a way of helping other people. "When the pandemic lockdowns started," Greer explained, "a writer friend said to me, 'I'm working on my novel, but it seems pointless with these protests over the George Floyd murder. I don't know if it's worth it to be a writer.' And I said, 'Pay attention. It's your job. You can pay attention to the details of pandemic life, or of the protest, or of absolutely anything.... [W]e need to be there, maybe not to create something that will help people right now but that will be of benefit to them later.'" When we notice the suffering of others as well as our own, a desire for other sentient beings to be happy can take root; instead of withdrawing from the world, we jump in.

The bardo rituals are a striking recognition of this kind of interdependence, of the individual as part of the collective and the collective as part of the individual. Because the rituals are meant to guide both the living and the dead, they affirm the relationship among us all as individuals who live and die. Sitting next to someone's dead body, we, the living, can see that one day, it will be *our* body laid out in the altar room. The person who has died, and the living who mourn her, are not different. We can't go home after the funeral and say, "Thank goodness that won't happen to me!" Because it will. In paying close, compassionate attention to impermanence, the bardo rituals help us acknowledge it as our shared experience.

Human community was never far from my grandmother's mind. One of my favorite memories of the time I spent with her is when we would listen to the BBC on the antediluvian radio after dinner, the crackly announcers' voices bringing news of the world's affairs and upheavals into the snug room high in the Himalayas. Propping her short, wide feet on the wall next to the fire, my grandmother followed the broadcast intently, brow knitted. Did I think Ronald Reagan was going to be a good president, she wanted to know, and what was my view of Margaret

Thatcher? It was terrible about the Haitian refugee crisis and the famine in Ethiopia.

My grandmother was greatly affected by the suffering of others and wanted to do something to help. "We Buddhists feel pain for all these people," she said. She prayed for everyone who was enduring political oppression and poverty and starvation, for the Tibetans who'd "lost so much at the hand of the Chinese," for everyone who had died a miserable death. She was always aware of her connection to both the living and the dead, of the human and spiritual ecology we're all a part of.

~

We tend to think of reality as monolithic: We know it exists and we know what it is. But what we pay attention to determines the nature of our reality. Although we're always paying attention, the question is: To what? Once we realize that what we perceive depends on what we focus on, we can direct our attention in ways that expand and deepen our engagement with the world around us, whether we pay attention to the winter rain or a hawk gliding in the sky or the suffering of others.

"O nobly-born, listen with full attention, without being distracted," *The Tibetan Book of the Dead* urges us. Rather than housekeeping in a dream, allowing ourselves to be spirited away in a never-ending parade of thoughts and reveries, we can exist in this moment, which is all we ever have anyway. Instead of diminishing our happiness by being distracted, we can develop a new awareness of our inner and outer worlds that allows us to live fully here, now.

# 5.
# TAKING BARDO BY THE FORELOCK

All experience is preceded by mind, led by mind, made by mind.

—The Buddha, *Dhammapada*, 1

Whatever river you drink from, forgetting does not erase your past. It only hides what wrecks you carry into the next life.

—Melissa Febos, *Girlhood*

When the *tsipa* astrologer lama arrived at my grandmother's house to cast the death horoscope, it was the first time I'd heard of this kind of horoscope. In the Tibetan way of looking at the world, the practice made sense: One horoscope was drawn up for the bardo journey from birth to death, and another for the voyage from death to rebirth. The death horoscope was like a road map, intended to help my grandmother travel well in bardo by identifying the hindrances on her path. It was also meant to illuminate the difficulties that we, her loved ones, might encounter, since the belief is that when someone dies, the remaining family members may face demon attacks and other challenges.

A grizzled man wearing horn-rimmed glasses, the tsipa performed his calculations using my grandmother's birth date, astrological sign (Wood Serpent), and time of death. "The following is an account of the departed soul of a person whose name is…," he said, beginning the reading-out of the horoscope. He informed us of the most auspicious day for the cremation and special prayers that must be done, and we learned that my grandmother remained attached to four things in the realm of the living. "The first three are a red hat, a copper bowl, and a red dress," the tsipa said. Then, like a modern-day therapist in monk's robes, he told us that my grandmother's mind also lingered on an unresolved relationship with her daughter. In a way, this didn't surprise me: My mother and grandmother had often had a hard time understanding each other. But I found it extraordinary that an ancient divination ritual had produced something so contemporary and relevant to our family.

When the reading of the horoscope was complete, we returned to the altar room, where the prayers for my grandmother were continuing. Smoke from the butter lamps floated in shafts of sunlight, and the smell of frying spices wafted from the kitchen at the back of the house. Condolence callers filed in and out, offering incense and *khada* scarves.

I sat for a while and listened to the lamas' rhythmic chanting, imagining my grandmother drifting in the spirit world, the beautiful prayers coming through in the darkness to remind her she had not been forsaken. I mused on what the death horoscope said about an unresolved mother-daughter relationship and recalled my grandmother's stories about her stepmother: "That woman never wanted to give us anything! I was the bold sow who went forward to fight with her, as among the lot I was fat, chubby, and strong." I thought about my mother's struggles with my grandmother: "Even though I'm a doctor," my mother said, "she thinks all I'm good for is tidying the house!" And for years, my mother and I had been caught in the push-and-pull of Asian mother and American daughter. I was, she worried, "too American," overly fond of speaking my mind and lacking in filial piety.

It hadn't ever occurred to me that mother-daughter conflict could be passed down like hair color or height, but now I wondered. Was it my karma to follow our family pattern with my daughter? *The Tibetan Book of the Dead* tells us, "O nobly-born,... the fierce wind of *karma*, terrific and hard to endure, will drive thee onwards, from behind, in dreadful gusts." Was I fated to carry on a mother-daughter legacy that had lasted for three generations?

*It was my karma to win the prize. It was my karma to lose that job. It was my karma to not get along with my daughter.* Karma is often thought of as fate, where what happens in life is beyond our control. It's seen as "what goes around comes around," as "just deserts" meted out by a higher power to reward or punish us for our actions.

Two of my grandmother's preferred maxims were *What is to happen will happen* and *What is allotted cannot be blotted*. For a long time, I assumed she was talking about karma—in other words, fate—which was something I'd given a lot of thought to. Because of my parents' acrimonious split and the fact that most of my friends' parents were no longer married (there was a steep rise in divorce after California Governor Ronald Reagan signed the country's first no-fault divorce bill into law in 1969), I felt sure that I was destined for a broken marriage.

The solution was clear: I would never marry. I would live alone by the sea with a dog and write. While girls I knew daydreamed about wedding dresses and honeymoons, I sketched out designs for my house and pondered what breed of dog to get. When I fell in love with Paris during my gap year, I adjusted my plan: I'd live alone near the Seine with a dog and write.

A few weeks after I arrived in Tokyo from Darjeeling, I was invited to a party and things took a turn. I'd intended to stay home and read but I felt lonely, so I threw on a little black dress and ventured out into the cold, rainy March night. Two hours and three train lines later, I reached the concrete apartment block in the suburbs where the gathering was being held.

Standing by the door when I walked in was a tall man with glasses, gray-green eyes, and brown hair, the bookish good looks I found so attractive. His name was David, and he'd come to Japan to teach English before starting a PhD program in anthropology. Witty, irreverent, brilliant, he regaled me with tales of life in Tokyo for *gaijin*, or us foreigners. We talked for most of the evening, then caught the last train back to the city and exchanged phone numbers.

Soon we were spending all our time together. We went to art house cinemas, live music clubs, and hole-in-the-wall restaurants where I ate unfamiliar foods like octopus, eel, and fermented soybeans. We took Japanese lessons, laughing over our mistakes (I asked a shopkeeper if I could pay in goldfish, *kingyō*, instead of cash, *genkin*) as we tried out our new knowledge. We saved up our money from teaching, then backpacked through Asia for three months, bicycling around the Dalai Lama's Norbulingka Palace in Lhasa, touring Nepal by motorcycle, and horseback riding in Burma. It was all more wonderful than I'd dreamed possible, but I still had no intention of getting married.

We returned to the States for graduate school, and one day about a year later, David asked me to marry him. To my surprise, I said yes. I was in love, and hopeful that I could give karma the slip. We got married on a sultry August afternoon at a bed-and-breakfast in rural New York. Relatives and friends flew in from around the world, including my grandmother, then eighty-three, who came all the way from Darjeeling. ("That airplane company must fly very slowly," she said, "because it took a long time to get here.") I wore a strapless organza dress, and David and I exchanged vows under a traditional blue-and-white Tibetan tent; at the end of the ceremony, my grandmother gave us each a khada scarf. I'd prepared a going-away outfit, but David and I were having such a good time that we stayed on, waving goodbye to the last guests after midnight.

For eight years, we enjoyed our life as graduate students and then as professors in Tokyo, traveling the world and uninterested in giving up our freedom to have children.

My indifference to motherhood was also related to a second decision I'd made as a girl: I would never become a mother, because I knew I was doomed to have smart-mouthed, disrespectful kids. *As you sow you shall reap* was another of my grandmother's favorite sayings, uttered in connection with children who lacked filial piety, like me. And my mother often said, "I just hope your own children don't treat you like this!" when I talked back to her. My worry was intensified by the cautionary tales I'd grown up with: a neighborhood mother who became an alcoholic, a friend's mother who kept trying to burn down the house.

As my thirty-fifth birthday approached, though, I changed my mind, unexpectedly aware that my childbearing years were passing. I soon got pregnant, but apprehension consumed me. I dreamed of crimson flowers growing on my grave as my mother and I stood side by side gazing at it. "You're buried there," my mother said. I dreamed I was locked in a house with my mother, desperate to escape and catch the first flight to Tokyo. As I neared my due date, my mother wrote me a letter: "I'm sure you're anxious to deliver, but I want to assure you that once the baby comes, you'll have little or no time, so you should enjoy this period. You don't know how a baby changes your life." I tried to encourage myself: *You've been happily married for almost a decade, so you dodged karma once. There's nothing at all to fear.* Maybe I'd get lucky and sidestep karma again—the way you might leap out of the path of an oncoming freight train.

On a May night in Tokyo, I gave birth to a little girl. As we lay together in the hospital, the moon sailing over the leafy trees in the park outside, I was overcome with joy. I felt sure that things would be different, that I could write my own story as a mother.

But in the what-is-allotted-cannot-be-blotted karmic payback I'd dreaded, my daughter, Sophia, turned out to be fiercely independent and strong-willed. She screamed and threw things, demanded reasons and explanations. I turned to books for help, my usual fallback as a writer, and learned that my daughter was "spirited," "sensitive," "passionate," and "high energy."

*Give your child positive reinforcement,* one expert advised. I made a chart to stick gold stars on when Sophia was a good girl; in red crayon, she drew a chart to put stars on when I was nice to her and taped it on the wall next to mine.

*Channel your child's determination by giving her choices.* "Do you want to wear your blue shirt or your orange shirt today?" I asked one morning, in a hurry to drop my daughter off at nursery school so I could get to work on time. "Neither one!" she shouted and raced off naked down the hallway.

I made lists and put them in the kitchen, the bathroom, the bedroom, to remind myself to stay calm in the heat of the moment (*Speak in your normal tone, redirect your child, don't get in a power struggle*). But entangled in the karma I should have known would find me sooner or later, I scolded and yelled, ordered Sophia to take time-outs she refused to take, and wished she would just behave.

My belief that karma meant inexorable fate began to change as I learned more about Buddhism. I came to understand that karma is about the principle of causality, where something can't arise from nothing. This idea is related to the concept of reincarnation, which holds that we're part of a continuum, with our past lives leading to this one.

The current Dalai Lama, for example, is believed to be the fourteenth incarnation in a line extending back to the 1300s, and before that, to Chenrezig, Bodhisattva of Compassion. After the Thirteenth Dalai Lama died in 1933, the search party tested the little boy thought to be his reincarnation by showing him a collection of items (a drum, spectacles, prayer beads), some of which had been used by the Thirteenth. The boy not only recognized his predecessor's belongings, but also had some of the physical characteristics (large ears, a tiger skin pattern on his legs) that, according to tradition, identify a Dalai Lama. Only four years old, he was brought to Lhasa from eastern Tibet. My grandmother told me, "When he arrived, he said, 'Not to the winter palace, take me to the summer palace.' Well, the

Potala Palace must have been cold, with over a thousand rooms you're shivering your head off. He didn't like that. But Norbulingka is bright, with a nice garden."

I knew about reincarnation in relation to the Dalai Lamas, but I'd never thought of it as having much to do with my everyday existence. One evening, though, when Sophia was a small girl and I was reading *Goodnight Moon* to her, she lay on her back staring at the ceiling, not listening to the story. "Before, that place where I lived was very big!" she said. Gesturing with her chubby hands, she described a house with plush drapery, people in every room, comfortable chairs and sofas.

When Henry was little, he talked of rebirth as a given. "What happens when I'm in my new skin?" he asked during lunch one day at a neighborhood ramen shop. "What I could come back as?" I'd also heard him mumbling the Buddhist mantra *om mani padme hum*, though we'd never said anything about it to him.

Regardless of what we believe or have experienced in relation to past lives, we can think of causality and reincarnation in terms of our previous selves—not whether you were a nineteenth-century Parisian cabaret singer or a forest monk on the Gangetic Plain in the Buddha's time, but who you were as a child, in high school, and so on, and how this has led to who you are now.

According to the Buddhist law of karma, or cause and effect, every result has a source or origin. The law accords to some extent with the idea of fate, except that "karma" (from the Sanskrit *karman,* or *kamma* in Pali) means "act." In a 2017 tweet to his millions of followers, the Dalai Lama said, "Karma means action...To complain that what happens to you is just the result of your karma is lazy. Instead, confidently recalling the advice that, 'You are your own master,' you can change what happens by taking action." At my grandmother's funeral, Rinpoche gave me advice that accorded with this, saying that we create our luck ourselves. "People want luck but they don't do anything to possess it," he explained. "We get it through beneficial activities of body, mind, and speech."

Karma is about how we shape our path through what we do, think, and say in each moment. This suggests "everything happens for a reason" logic, except the reason comes from us, not something outside ourselves. If our actions are positive, that's all to the good, but if not, we make ourselves miserable through habitual behavior that is, in Buddhist terms, "unskillful": getting into power struggles with your child, having the same pointless arguments with your partner, staying silent when you should speak up. As *The Tibetan Book of the Dead* tells us, "O nobly-born,...listen. That thou art suffering so cometh from thine own *karma*; it is not due to anyone else's."

Rather than looking inward, we tend to believe that the only way we can be happy is if things in our environment change (if only my daughter would be a good girl, if only my boss would take me seriously). We wait and hope for external transformation to occur, but—even though change is the fundamental truth of life—in this respect things unfortunately tend to stay the same.

Our actions shape our path by influencing our perceptions. A person who envies others is inclined to experience life as a zero-sum game. A fearful person tends to perceive interactions as threatening and aggressive. One of my favorite illustrations of how perspective—actions of mind—forms perception is a point-of-view writing exercise in John Gardner's *The Art of Fiction*:

> Describe a landscape as seen by an old woman whose disgusting and detestable old husband has just died. Do not mention the husband or death.
>
> Describe a lake as seen by a young man who has just committed murder. Do not mention the murder.
>
> Describe a landscape as seen by a bird. Do not mention the bird.

Think about how you would describe your kitchen, or people at the supermarket, if you were grieving or angry. Now imagine how the same scene would look if you were in love. In this way, our actions guide what we perceive.

When Henry was about seven, he joined a soccer club. One day I picked him up after a game and asked how his team had done. He replied, "I think we lost." Friendship and camaraderie mattered more to him than competition; he didn't perceive the world in terms of winners and losers. (He loved *The Story of Ferdinand*, a tale about a bull that would rather sit and smell flowers than fight in the ring.) For Henry, the game was a chance to hang out with his coach and teammates on a sunny fall afternoon. As a point-of-view writing exercise, this could be: "Describe a soccer game as seen by a player who cares more about human connection than competition."

The way we determine our path with our actions of body, mind, and speech is a concept with huge power. What's happening now is a consequence of your actions last year, last week, yesterday, and this morning, and all of that, plus what you do now, will lead to results in the future. In other words, we're continuously engaged in the creation of our reality—not in the sense of influencing things that are beyond our control (it wasn't up to my grandmother whether or not my grandfather died), but in terms of choosing how we act (accepting her husband's death made it easier for my grandmother to grieve).

Though we may feel frustration and despair, loneliness and sorrow, in the situations we encounter in life, we have choice in what we do, think, and say, and in this sense, we shape both our present and our future. Until we recognize the relationship between our actions and the path we take, we go around and around in *samsara* suffering.

In *Buddha*, a history of the Buddha and his teachings, Karen Armstrong says that during Prince Gautama's time (before he became the Buddha), "the prospect of living one life after another filled [Gautama], like most other people in northern India, with horror." In our day-to-day existence, "living one life after another" can be understood as repeating unskillful behavior over and over. Releasing yourself from this cycle means beginning to change whatever is causing you misery through new actions of body, mind, and speech.

My grandmother's death horoscope said that her life force had begun to diminish in the eighth month of the Tibetan calendar, September, but she'd lived until the end of November because of her positive actions, or karma. The horoscope identified hindrances arising from any negative karma she might have accumulated and determined astrological remedies to help overcome them. The remedies required the skull of a pig with its lips and ears, a white horse skull, a red horse carrying water, a magpie, and a turquoise stone.

How, I wondered, might such objects be found? Sometimes the deceased wandered for ages in bardo, unable to escape samsara and only taking rebirth in one of the lower realms, as an animal, a hungry ghost, or a hell being—Was the horoscope indicating this would happen to my grandmother if the remedies couldn't be carried out?

The tsipa assured us, though, that if the specified items weren't readily available, they could be drawn, and if no one could draw, why, we could imagine them. In any event, he continued, my grandmother's beneficial actions during her lifetime would be of great help to her in bardo, just as skillful actions can help us travel well through the bardo between birth and death.

"Happiness and misery will depend upon *karma*," *The Tibetan Book of the Dead* instructs, reminding us of the causal relationship between our actions and how we experience life. In bardo, the book tells us, those "who have accumulated merit, and devoted themselves sincerely to religion, will experience various delightful pleasures and happiness and ease in full measure." For people with bad karma, however, the outlook is bleak: "In...cases of persons of much evil *karma*, *karmically*-produced flesh-eating *rākshasas* [or demons] bearing various weapons will utter, 'Strike! Slay!' and so on, making a frightful tumult.... [H]allucinations of being pursued by many people likewise will come; [and] sounds as of mountains crumbling down, and of angry overflowing seas, and of the roaring of fire."

## TAKING BARDO BY THE FORELOCK

If you're short on merit, you might find yourself called up in front of Yama, Lord of Death, and his tribunal of fearsome animal-headed demons and deities. His court assembles with much shuffling and bumping and snorting, impassive eyes staring out from furry, macabre faces. As you beg to be spared the consequences of your actions, Yama's hideous attendants snicker and snort; the spectators in the gallery rock with laughter.

Yama has a mirror (your memory), as well as a scale to weigh white pebbles (good deeds) against black pebbles (evil deeds). *The Tibetan Book of the Dead* tells us:

> Thereupon, thou wilt be greatly frightened, awed, and terrified, and wilt tremble; and thou wilt attempt to tell lies, saying, "I have not committed any evil deed."
> Then the Lord of Death will say, "I will consult the Mirror of *Karma*."
> So saying, he will look in the Mirror, wherein every good and evil act is vividly reflected. Lying will be of no avail.
> Then one of the Executive Furies of the Lord of Death will place round thy neck a rope and drag thee along; he will cut off thy head, extract thy heart, pull out thy intestines, lick up thy brain, drink thy blood, eat thy flesh, and gnaw thy bones.

# TRAVELING IN BARDO

In a footnote, Evans-Wentz elaborates:

> These tortures symbolize the pangs of the deceased's conscience.... One element... of the consciousness-content of the deceased, comes forward, and, by offering lame excuses, tries to meet accusations against it, saying, "Owing to such-and-such circumstances I had to do so-and-so." Another element of the consciousness-content comes forward and says, "You were guided by such-and-such motives; your deeds partake of the black colour." Then some more friendly one of such elements arises and protests, "But I have such-and-such justification; and the deceased deserves pardon on these grounds." And so—as the *lāmas* explain—the Judgement proceeds.

In the mirror, you might see yourself letting a call from a friend in need go to voicemail, running over the neighbor's dog by accident and driving away, lying to your partner (or yourself) about having an affair. Essentially, this part of the teaching is about recognizing that we are the ones who decide what we do, think, and say, and we should own this. If you make excuses and refuse to take responsibility for your actions, my grandmother used to tell me, "There'll be *boiling* waiting, devils with a noose there to eat your brains and drag you off. In hot, boiling oil you're thrown and your body is roasted. With all the burns, you're finished." Having consigned yourself to the hell of blaming what happens in your life on other people and external circumstances, you will suffer unceasingly.

In the bardo from birth to death, the reckoning symbolized by Yama and his tribunal may occur as our last day approaches, or at moments in life—the end of a relationship, the death of a loved one—when we come face to face with our unskillful behavior and its consequences.

In traditional Tibetan belief, generating positive karma—merit through skillful actions—for benefit both in your present life and your lives to come is very important. This is illustrated by a story in the biography of my great-grandfather, Laden La, about how he solved a diplomatic imbroglio in a town near Darjeeling while doing police work in 1907:

> The Tibetan Minister, Tsarong Shape, visited Kalimpong, and reported that a large sum of money, namely Rs.3,000 in silver, had been stolen from him on his first night there. He was furious, and very influential, and the police had a big problem on their hands. Communal trouble was a strong possibility. [Laden La] arrived in Kalimpong within hours, and rapidly assessed the situation. He guessed that the thief

was probably a local Buddhist, and he persuaded the lamas to conduct a puja [prayer ceremony] that threatened dire retribution on the miscreants, both in this life and in future lives, and the fact of the upcoming puja was widely publicised. The day before the puja was to take place, the amount of Rs.2,882 was quietly returned, and everyone was happy.

Laden La's solution to the crisis isn't surprising, because gaining karmic merit was one of his guiding principles, motivating him to act according to Buddhist virtues such as generosity, compassion, and ethical conduct. He established the Himalayan Children's Advancement Association, which found homes for hundreds of orphans, and was president of the Hillmen's Association, an organization that worked for greater sovereignty for the Darjeeling hill people. He took four Tibetan boys to be educated in England at the request of the Thirteenth Dalai Lama, and in addition to facilitating the translation of the *Bardo Thödol*, he was a patron of many local monasteries. My grandmother kept an autograph book for friends, family, and visitors to sign and delighted in showing everyone what her father had written in his flowing hand:

> A loving heart is the great requirement!
> To regard the people as an only son;

not to oppress, not to destroy; not to exalt oneself by treading down others, but to comfort and befriend those in suffering.
To think no evil and do none: on the contrary, to benefit all creatures.

Like her father, my grandmother endeavored to do good deeds, opening a Red Cross office in her house in the 1940s to recruit women for the war effort and caring for wounded soldiers sent up from the Burma front to convalesce; supporting the Tibetan Refugee Self-Help Centre; looking after young Western women who arrived in Darjeeling, frightened and strung out on drugs, sometimes pregnant. And my grandfather was such a principled man, she liked to remember, that he surely went straight to a fine rebirth after he died. "Everyone said that in his thirty-eight years as an honorary magistrate, there had never been someone of that caliber," she told me. "People used to come to the house offering butter, meat, and he used to return those gifts. He said, 'Full justice will be done, but I don't want anything from you.' There was never any hanky-panky."

In the Tibetan custom, virtuous activities day-to-day are complemented by pilgrimage, a powerful means of gaining karmic merit. When you go on pilgrimage, you step away from routine existence to journey to sacred spots, cultivating positive imprints in your mind as you pray and make offerings and reflect on the wisdom associated with the sites that you visit. When you return home and reenter ordinary life, your transformed perspective inspires you to carry out further beneficial actions.

For centuries, Tibetans have set off on pilgrimage to places such as Mount Kailash, believed to be the *axis mundi* and to have been blessed by Guru Rinpoche, and nearby Lake Manasarovar, where sea yaks and sea sheep are said to dwell in the blue waters and where, according to legend, Queen Maya bathed before giving birth to Gautama, the Buddha. You might leave your family for one or two years, or go in a truck with pots and pans and tents and return in a month. (If you're too busy or lazy or old, or worried about personal safety, you can hire someone to go in your place.)

When my grandmother rode her pony to Tibet, one of the dandy wallahs' wives made the journey on foot. "Her husband was carrying the dandy, the palanquin, and with him, side by side, she was walking," my grandmother said. "We told her, 'Get on a pony back there, we'll let you have one.' She said, 'Nothing doing.' She walked all the way up and then back down to Darjeeling, hundreds of miles. Going to Lhasa walking, or prostrating the whole way, taking all the trouble, you're earning merit."

In addition to leading groups of Buddhists on annual pilgrimage to Tso Pema, the lake where Guru Rinpoche performed miracles, my great-grandfather went on pilgrimage with the Thirteenth Dalai Lama when His Holiness took refuge in Darjeeling in 1910. They traveled to Bodh Gaya, where the Buddha reached enlightenment under a bodhi tree, and other holy sites. My grandmother continued her father's tradition with her own family: Every year, she and my grandfather took my mother and her siblings on winter pilgrimage to the places where the Buddha walked—Varanasi, Bodh Gaya, Sarnath.

My mother loved falling asleep to the sound of the train and waking up at dawn in the vast plains, seeing the wildfowl and village life. The family would give food and money to the poor, and light butter lamps and pray in the monasteries and temples. "The prayers are not only for yourself and your relations, but for all the living creatures of the world," my grandmother used to tell me. "Whatever we do while we are alive, we are earning credit for the next birth. I think the Buddhist religion is a very good religion. You do all the good you can, in all the ways you can, in all the places you can."

~

Its taproot descending to the wisdom and practices of ancient times, the idea of karma has permeated contemporary American culture. John Lennon sang about it in "Instant Karma! (We All Shine On)," the Beatles' first single to sell a million copies, released after they traveled to Rishikesh, India, in 1968 to study Transcendental Meditation. Over fifty years later, "Karma," a 2022 song by Taylor Swift, has been streamed hundreds of millions of times. (In a *Vogue* interview, Swift was asked, "What do you think is the most important life lesson for someone to learn?" She replied, "That karma is real.")

Popular as the idea of karma is, as we learn more about it, we may feel overwhelmed by the fact that we're responsible for our reality, that not only is what's happening now a result of our past actions, but we can change our present and future at this very moment. "Be not afraid," *The Tibetan Book of the Dead* instructs, exhorting us to "take bardo by the forelock" rather than allow the reverse to happen.

We often feel at the mercy of what life brings, but in the same way that the traveler in the after-death bardo decides her trajectory with her choices—the sooner she admits she's dead, for instance, the sooner she can move forward—we influence what happens for us through what we do, or don't do, in the face of "what is." Understanding the true meaning of karma is liberating rather than threatening. It gives us more control over our lives and therefore greater contentment, which is, after all, what we seek.

In a way, it's easy. If you don't want what usually happens to happen, do something different. In other words, stop doing things that make you unhappy. But even when our habitual actions bring us misery, we too often repeat them again and again, like the unfortunate, single-minded pigeons conditioned to peck at a target in B. F. Skinner's famous experiment. We do this until something or someone, like we ourselves, disrupts the cycle. The good news is that, as difficult as it may seem to change our actions, we can transform what isn't working for us through incremental shifts in our everyday activities of body, mind, and speech.

You might start by identifying an action you engage in that makes you suffer. It could be something you do or think or say at work, or when you're by yourself or with your friends, partner, or children. Perhaps you take on too many tasks at the office, gossip about colleagues, procrastinate. When you're alone, you obsess over the latest headlines and social media posts, worrying about everything from the state of the world to whether other people's lives are better than yours. You may be troubled by a conflict between your values and your behavior: You care about kindness but exclude a friend from a dinner party, lose your temper with your partner and say things you regret, belittle your child.

One common unskillful behavior is negative self-talk. *How could you be so stupid? You never get anything right. You're a failure.* This action disposes us toward more negative self-talk, and so it goes, on and on, shaping the way we see ourselves and the world (and how the world sees us), and making us unhappy. To transform this behavior once we've identified it, we can practice encouraging ourselves just as we would reassure our children, or a friend, taking to heart what the Buddha taught about compassion as the desire for everyone, including ourselves, to be free of suffering.

If we fall into self-criticism, we can do something different in that very moment. Instead of "You should have known better," you can say, "You did your best knowing what you knew." "You never get anything right" can become "Things didn't go as you hoped, but no worries, you can try again." Growing aware of negative self-talk and changing it to positive reassurance is a simple, powerful way to disrupt the unskillful habit and create new karmic imprints for our trajectory going forward. By changing an action that doesn't serve us, we not only change our experience in the moment, but lay the ground for making different choices in the future.

In another illustration of the way that incremental change can have life-altering consequences, author Melissa Febos told me in a conversation for my bardo interview series how she stopped seeking approval from others:

> Because I'd grown up as a girl in the United States of America, I felt for a long time that it was important not to make other people uncomfortable by

asserting my physical boundaries. When I finally stopped to interrogate this, I realized I had to slow down my reactions until the moment where I could make a choice became visible. When someone said, "Let's hug," I had to step back and wait a few beats—very awkward—for the moment when I could discern whether I wanted to. Oftentimes, the answer was no.... The important part is that moment of pause where, instead of looking outward to assess what the other person wants, I listen inward to what *I* want.

Through minute examination of her actions of body, mind, and speech, Febos changed what appeared to be her fate as a girl in American society.

At any point during the journey through bardo, we can go up toward an enlightened state or down toward the realms of rebirth in samsara suffering. The "ever-moving wind of *karma*," says *The Tibetan Book of the Dead*, drives us forward: Our actions now are conditioned by our prior actions. The more we choose the positive (honesty, compassion), or, conversely, the negative (lying, criticizing others and ourselves), the more likely we are to keep acting in these ways. It's up to us whether, as my grandmother used to say, we end up "a timid worm, a money-minded ant, a dog pulling its tongue out with jealousy," slogging on through trials of our own making, or move into an awakened way of living. At each moment, we have choice. Instead of tending the same old garden, we can till the soil for a new one, planting seeds and letting them flourish.

~

It's easy to believe that the past vanishes if we don't think about it, but it only fades from our sight. Elena Pakhoutova, senior curator of Himalayan art at the Rubin Museum, has written about the significance of the past in the HBO series *Westworld*. The series depicts androids at a Western-themed amusement park whose memories are erased every time they finish acting out a scenario with the human visitors. But an android named Dolores starts trying to change. "Dolores struggles to remember her past," Pakhoutova says, "as she is programmed to experience her life in the park over and over again, forgetting each time it begins anew. This cycle is similar to living out your karma until this karma is exhausted and something new develops, or a new state of consciousness begins."

When I returned home to Tokyo after my grandmother's funeral, I pondered what her death horoscope said about an unresolved mother-daughter relationship. I thought for the first time in a long while about the family patterns that had surfaced around my wedding. My father and some other family members decided not to come, a deeply wounding but unsurprising rupture along the fault lines created by decades of strife between my parents. Another absence that devastated me was of a close friend and mentor who'd helped me through some very difficult times. Not long before the wedding, she killed herself, following in the footsteps of her mother and grandmother. On the phone with her husband, I wept over the loss of such a beautiful soul and over the inheritance she'd been unable to free herself from. When I told him about the split in my family, he said, "Well, the challenge for you is to break the pattern with your own children."

Since I'd never intended to have children, I'd forgotten that conversation. But after my grandmother died, it came back to me. Knowing about the mother-daughter legacy that had endured in my family for generations, but not doing whatever I could to change it, would be like hearing that a hurricane was forecast and sitting idly on the porch hoping the storm would turn off course. I thought about how, growing up in Darjeeling, my mother disliked the way that, for my grandmother, boys always came first and girls were "second-class citizens." When the children were given presents and money at *Losar* New Year, my mother's brothers each got one-third, and she and her two sisters had to share the remaining third. The girls were expected to be "good housegirls"—organize the photos in albums, polish the silver—regardless of their intelligence or achievements. If you were "bold" like she was, my mother said, you were "squelched."

When my mother arrived in New York in 1951, the first Tibetan to study medicine in America, she was excited to be an up-to-the-minute young woman casting off old-world customs. She gave a press conference at the Look Building in Manhattan and told the reporters, "I am an enlightened girl. I'm all for anything modern!" When she wasn't in class or at the lab, she popped out with friends for dinner at the Tip Toe Inn or a drink and a smoke at Monkey Bar; to parties where "girls talked freely to boys in a very natural way," she wrote to her parents, something that was simply not done in Darjeeling. Her roommates were "typical American girls who put a high priority on their independence, an attitude which I am beginning to find sensible."

Yet once my mother became a mother herself, she held to the traditional expectations believed to ensure a girl's future success, just as her own mother had. When, to her consternation, I turned out to be a bold girl—by nature, coming of age during the era of Betty Friedan and Gloria Steinem, and encouraged by my father to consider myself anyone's equal—she fretted that I was "intense" and a "troublemaker," just like my father (people who didn't question authority were the real troublemakers, my father insisted). She worried that, given my penchant for backtalk, no one would want to marry me, which I didn't see as a problem since I wasn't planning to get married.

One of the things my daughter Sophia loved to do as a small girl was march around the house swinging a plastic sword and belting out *Mulan* battle songs. Now, aware of our mother-daughter legacy, I wondered how to honor her determination and drive, not cast us as adversaries. As I puzzled and brainstormed, I tried to be more conscious of my habitual actions, especially at times that felt like forks in the road that would determine the direction of our relationship.

A moment like this occurred one summer morning when I took the children to Tama Zoo in western Tokyo to see the koalas, an excursion they'd been looking forward to for days. As we entered the Australian Zone and approached the koala enclosure, Sophia spotted a few koalas curled up in a tree, furry gray balls bearing little resemblance to the cute koalas in her picture books. "Why are they all sleeping?" she asked. When I explained that they're nocturnal, she started shouting: "What's the point of coming if they just sleep all day?" "What a waste of time!" "Why didn't you check beforehand?"

Things I could say, that I'd heard so often as a child, popped into my head with frightening speed: *We're leaving now, you ungrateful girl. You've ruined our special outing. You'll stay home next time.*

Fighting anger and frustration, I said, "It's so disappointing, isn't it? I wanted to see the koalas awake too!" Henry nodded, "Me too." We commiserated over vanilla soft serves at a nearby snack stand, then went in search of the lions.

Rather than wishing Sophia were an easier child, I started thinking more about what was going on inside her. When she lashed out, it was usually because she was being buffeted by gale-force emotions over things like the arrival of her baby brother, trouble balancing on her bike without training wheels, not being invited to a birthday party that all her friends had gone to. She wasn't difficult; she was a young person in need of guidance. And we weren't fated to have a fraught relationship—with our actions in the here and now, we could break the cycle.

I think often about the belief that the death horoscope can benefit the surviving relations. The horoscope isn't about simply hoping for change, but about what we can *do* in the face of whatever arises in the bardo between birth and death. We can't control what happens, but we can take responsibility for our actions as we navigate the challenges that life inevitably brings. Just as the astrologer lama's forecast named the hindrances my grandmother would encounter in bardo and remedies for overcoming them, it helped me recognize and seek to vanquish the demons on my path. It showed me that although I can't change the past, I can work to change what takes place now and in the days ahead, for me and my daughter as well as for the generations to come.

There was also a way in which the death horoscope could help me redress the ills suffered by the older generations of my family. Throughout her long life, my grandmother carried the pain of how her stepmother had treated her. And she worried that her *lungta*, her luck, was being pulled down by my mother's annoyance at being asked to do things like sort through the books in the study or inventory the dinnerware. As for my mother, she has never gotten over her resentment at my grandmother's attitude toward girls, especially because this dynamic continued into adulthood and old age. ("Even if the mother is ninety and the daughter is seventy," my grandmother used to say, "the mother has every right to tell the daughter what to do.") And determined as my mother was to raise me as an American, she didn't realize this would mean I wouldn't listen to her in the way she hoped and expected. ("Who do you think you are?" she'd say when we locked horns.)

I hear my grandmother's and my mother's voices:

> *That stepmother never wanted to give us anything.*
> *I'm on pins and needles with your mother.*
> *The boys always came first.*
> *Who do you think you are?*

Iron-willed women who made lives of their own, my grandmother and my mother were free in some ways but not free in others. Each one loved the life she was living—my grandmother as a hotel owner, my mother as a physician in California—but their unsettled feelings about mother and daughter persisted and, instinctively, they sought to remedy this.

My grandmother was keen to tell me about the struggles she'd endured growing up. Whenever I was in Darjeeling, she would come find me and say, "What else would you like to know?" And my mother recounted many stories over the years, as well as gave me the letters that she and her parents had exchanged after her departure for America. In my youth, I'd felt a deep sense of unfairness, just like my grandmother and my mother had—Did they sense I would understand? Did they pass their stories down to me so that, as a writer, I could tell a new story for them, and for me and my daughter?

When you know a story, you have the chance to change it, for yourself and the people you love. Have you noticed patterns in your family that repeat across generations? Is there a relative who can share her stories with you and shed light on these patterns? We can reach back and seize our family stories, bring them into the present. A dialogue between generations can take place, either through actual conversations now or through recovered diaries, letters, objects, and photographs. "Generation" refers to the people in a given age group, but I love the other meaning: production, as in inception, initiation, and summoning forth. As we do this work of excavation, patterns emerge, and we can decide which ones to keep and which to let go of.

Drawing family patterns into the light of day may seem unappealing. Why revive old ghosts? But the ghosts of our past are alive and well, whether or not we acknowledge them. And as the bardo teachings remind us, although the past is always reverberating in our lives, it doesn't have to dictate the present or the future.

Karma as family repair extends beyond our personal circumstances into our communities, both locally and globally. As we take responsibility for how the past has led to our present individual reality, we become more receptive to identifying and exploring historical, intergenerational patterns in society, and to working to enact cultural repair. We can recognize and change the patterns that reproduce injustice, and preserve the ones that are vibrant and positive. This possibility has powerful implications for the challenges we face today, such as racial discrimination and gender violence, climate change and biodiversity loss, where the actions that we take now will determine the future of humanity and our planet.

In his introduction to *The Tibetan Book of the Dead*, Evans-Wentz explains that when we emancipate ourselves from the samsara cycle of suffering, we experience "the

Ending of Sorrow." This doesn't mean an end to the difficulties we inevitably encounter in the bardo of life, but to the misery we bring upon ourselves through our actions of body, mind, and speech.

Working toward a different kind of relationship with my daughter has not only led me to feel more at peace, it's opened me up to the positive connections between generations. This was brought home when I returned to Darjeeling for the ceremony by the Teesta River the year after my grandmother died. One day, I walked with my mother to my grandmother's house, clouds shape-shifting over the valleys in the spring breeze. My grandmother's helper welcomed us in a stream of affectionate Nepali and ushered us to the living room, where the usual teatime items had been laid out with painstaking care: the teapot and embroidered cozy; the gleaming silver sugar bowl and creamer of heated milk; the Wedgwood Campion flower-patterned china. Over cucumber sandwiches and freshly brewed first flush from the local Makaibari Tea Estate, my mother and I talked of this and that, the sound of car horns drifting up from the Hill Cart Road through the clerestory windows.

After tea, we sorted through things in the house, and then we went to the altar room because my mother wanted to light incense for my grandmother. On the altar were the butter lamps and silver bowls of water that my grandmother's helper continued to offer every morning; dust motes floated in the late afternoon sunshine. "The weather was so beautiful on the day of your grandmother's funeral, and again today," my mother said as she held an incense stick in the flame of a butter lamp. "Your grandmother is obviously pleased we've come."

My grandmother would indeed have been happy to see her daughter and granddaughter together at the family altar. As I watched my mother swirl the incense in front of the statue of Guru Rinpoche, I realized that this ritual of continuity would have troubled me when I thought I was fated to repeat negative mother-daughter patterns. Now, holding my own incense stick in the flame of the butter lamp, I felt the love and strength that was also part of my family's mother-daughter legacy. This, then, was how it would go: Just as my grandmother prayed for the mother she'd lost as a small girl, my mother now offered incense for her mother, and, when my mother was gone, somewhere, in some way, I would do the same for her, and when I was gone, my daughter for me.

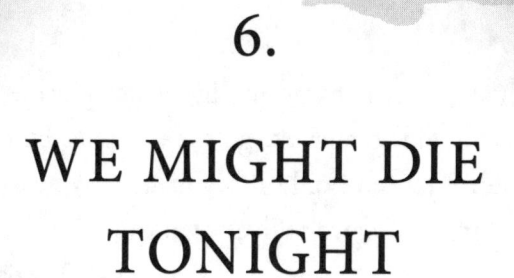

# 6.

# WE MIGHT DIE TONIGHT

My religion is to live—and die—without regret.

—Milarepa

Best advice I ever got was an old friend of mine, a black friend, who said you have to go the way your blood beats. If you don't live the only life you have, you won't live some other life, you won't live any life at all.

—James Baldwin

At dawn outside Lhasa, a *rogyapa* body-breaker flays a human corpse on a rocky outcropping as shrieking, hissing vultures swoop down to devour the remains. Monks seated nearby read from *The Tibetan Book of the Dead*, guiding the dead person through bardo. Juniper smoke swirls in the thin air of the high plateau and the sun rises over the surrounding mountains. The rogyapa, a woman in dark clothing and apron, bends over the corpse, holding what looks like a shin bone. The body has mostly been dismembered—you can see ribs, a head of hair. The rogyapa slices away the flesh and hammers at the bones, chatting and bantering with the male rogyapa working alongside her. Methodically, they proceed with their task. By the end of the ritual, the vultures have consumed the flesh and organs, along with the bones that have been crushed and mixed with *tsampa* barley flour.

When my great-grandfather was in Tibet in the 1920s, he took this picture, one of the earliest records of a traditional sky burial. Perhaps my grandmother, then a teenager, was at his side, helping with the photographic plates and other equipment while observing the ritual. Throughout her life, westerners would ask her why Tibetans practiced the "barbaric" sky burial custom—Wasn't it all too gruesome and disturbing to watch?

## TRAVELING IN BARDO

"The way we think of it," she told me, "seeing the body chopped up, you realize that death is always there waiting, so no time to waste."

I thought about this as I watched my grandmother's body burn at her cremation, as flames consumed the coffin and my grandmother's blackened head came into view, facing toward mighty Kanchenjunga and Tibet. Tibetan birth horoscopes predict the age at which you'll die; I wondered if my grandmother had known what her horoscope foretold. I doubted, though, that she would have lived any differently even if the horoscope had indicated she'd live to one hundred and she'd been aware of that. For her, it was always as *The Tibetan Book of the Dead* taught—consciousness of death allows us to live a more meaningful life—and as the Dalai Lama says: "You must not procrastinate. Rather, you should make preparations so that even if you [died] tonight, you would have no regrets."

~

Stories of sudden death are common. Car accidents, strokes, plane crashes. Earthquakes, tsunamis, floods, fires. Friends, acquaintances, and strangers; famous people like Kobe Bryant, Natasha Richardson, James Gandolfini. A friend of mine in her forties had a heart attack when she was at home one evening with her husband and daughter.

She died so quickly, her husband told me, there wasn't even time to say goodbye. One day, my grandfather, a New Jersey physician, said to his wife, "Margaret, I think my heart has stopped," and died. My uncle was diagnosed with pancreatic cancer and hoped he had at least a few more months so he could put his affairs in order, but he only had two weeks. His roommate in the hospital was a handsome, middle-aged man who'd been on vacation with his wife in Cuba, caught a virus, and was dying. I'll never forget the shock and bewilderment on the man's face as he realized that his last moment had arrived.

There are other kinds of swift endings. One of my oldest friends, a Japanese woman I met when I arrived in Tokyo in 1985, came for lunch every month for twenty years. She took the same train from her place and walked the same route to my house from the station. She'd ring the bell a few minutes early, bearing fresh-baked pastries, a novel she'd just read, and, if she'd been traveling, a souvenir from London or Barcelona or Budapest. One afternoon, she was late. I'd been waiting for about half an hour when the police called—my friend had wandered in and given them my number.

"Are you all right?" I asked when they handed her the phone.

"No, not all right." She'd lost her way on the route she knew so well and ended up at the police station. That was the day her dementia began, when she was in her seventies, and she could no longer leave the house on her own.

Though we all know stories like these, we go through life "just spending our time," my grandmother used to say, in a kind of deep sleep where we're "more dead than alive." When our last moment comes, we're astonished. *What? There's so much I wanted to do, to be.* We regret that we settled for a life that was less than the one we'd dreamed of and we didn't pursue the happiness that could have been ours.

In *How Proust Can Change Your Life*, author Alain de Botton tells us that in 1922, the Paris newspaper *L'Intransigeant* asked Proust how he thought people would respond if they learned that a cataclysmic event would soon kill hundreds of millions of people. Proust replied,

> I think that life would suddenly seem wonderful to us if we were threatened to die as you say. Just think of how many projects, travels, love affairs, studies, it—our life—hides from us, made invisible by our laziness which, certain of a future, delays them incessantly.
>
> But let all this threaten to become impossible for ever, how beautiful it would become again! Ah! If only the cataclysm doesn't happen this time, we won't miss visiting the new galleries of the Louvre, throwing ourselves at the feet of Miss X, making a trip to India.

Yet, if the cataclysm doesn't occur, Proust said, we fall back into our usual indolence, forgetting the urgency that seized us when we thought our end was nigh, oblivious once more to the fact that we might expire this very evening.

Our daily routines lull us into feeling immortal. The tangibility of things casts a spell on us, the irrefutable physicality of the objects (the family silverware, a favorite necklace) and ordinary rituals (walking the dog, watering the garden, chopping vegetables for dinner) that we love. Helping my mother sort through her house when she moved to a retirement home, I came across sewing instructions for a pink wool tweed coat with jewel buttons, the libretto for Debussy's *Pelléas et Mélisande*, a recipe for fruit cobbler with "Delicious crust!" written on it in my mother's neat script.

My grandmother's diaries are filled with the same kind of materiality, the texture of normal life that so suffuses our sense of being we can't imagine it all suddenly ending. In an entry on an ordinary Wednesday in 2000 ("another lovely day"), my grandmother reports going up to the hotel to interview a prospective cook, to Ghoom Monastery to offer butter lamps, and then to a local shop to buy two Tibetan carpets as a wedding gift. After lunch, she rested for a while, then "got up to say prayers and do little things in the house."

Daily life enchants us, which is all to the good, but it can blind us to the reality that our end may come at any moment and there's no time to waste.

## TRAVELING IN BARDO

My grandmother's stories were often about sudden death:

> One fine day he was playing tennis, started coughing blood, and bang! He was gone.
> Her brother, born a reincarnate lama, came out of the womb in the meditation posture. Hair all like little ringlets. Next thing, he was dead of double pneumonia!

At tea, over gin and tonics, my grandmother would listen with a knowing air to her friends' death-related stories:

> The fellow is mad as a badger. His son, a nice, polished lad, got the call from upstairs and keeled over in the middle of a polo match.
> The poor chap pegged out on the spot, ill-treated by the wife. Carrying all her luggage told on his heart.

Was my grandmother's worldview oriented toward death because she'd experienced so much loss? Her mother had died instantly as she bowed down to the high lama, perhaps from a stroke. When my grandmother was in her thirties, her father passed away unexpectedly while campaigning in the nearby town of Kalimpong for a seat in the Bengal Legislative Assembly. "He was on the threshold of a new career and overnight, suddenly, a light was snuffed out," his biography recounts. My grandfather died in my grandmother's arms, and she outlived three of her five children. She witnessed the end of the Raj, the British rule of India, in 1947, and the crushing of Tibet by China in 1959. She spoke to me of friends who, after the Chinese took over, were stripped of everything. One such friend, a respected member of Lhasa society, "came down running" to India, dressed like a beggar to avoid capture; another from a prominent family died in prison in Tibet.

A devout Buddhist, my grandmother knew well that, as *The Tibetan Book of the Dead* says, we are all mortal and we don't know when the end will come. Perhaps, too, she talked about death because of her long familiarity with the traditional rituals that keep the dead close: sitting next to the body for days, washing and dressing it, lighting the pyre. In America, death is often held at a distance, with strangers hired to handle the tasks involved in seeing off the dead, but my grandmother developed a lexicon of loss through intimate acquaintance with death, a way of interacting with dying and death that not only helped her grieve but served as a reminder, again and again, that now is the time to live, that however much we may wring our hands over the past and speculate about the future, we can only exist in this moment.

## TRAVELING IN BARDO

Even though the fleeting nature of the world is scientific fact, and we know that people die every day, we put things off. *I'll do it later.* How often do we say this to ourselves? Later you'll move to Rome, write a play, spend more time with your children, work less (or more), tell your partner how much you love them, forgive so-and-so. Then, as the end approaches and we still haven't done all we hoped to do, we want one more day, one more hour.

When my father lay in the hospital in a coma, I felt sure that he had more time, that we had more time together. It was inconceivable that after eighty years, he might have only minutes left. The autumn sunshine of the Napa wine country spilled into the room, illuminating me, my sisters, and my father's best friend of over fifty years, as we stood in a circle around the bed. I felt like we were in one of the Vermeers I'd seen at the Louvre when I lived in Paris: the interplay of light and shadow, the photographic precision of my father's figure, the way parts of the painting were out of focus.

The doctor came by and I asked him why my father's ears were turning black.

"It's necrosis, because of diminished blood flow." A clean-cut, sincere man of about thirty, he wanted to do something for my father, "open him up and fix what's wrong," but the sepsis was too advanced. He talked about bowel obstruction, a high white blood cell count and low blood pressure, atropine to control my father's erratic heart rate, vasopressors to constrict his blood vessels. My father had been hypothermic when he came in, they couldn't do an arterial blood draw, he might have pancreatitis, he was acidotic. They were delivering 100 percent oxygen and had started him on broad-spectrum antibiotics, but his organs were shutting down. "Last night, he went into cardiac arrest," the doctor said, "and coded this morning. I'm surprised he made it back. We're recommending DNR. The prognosis…"

In the distance, the vineyards shimmered as the wind blew down from the Sierras to the sea. Except for the beeping of the heart monitor, we might have been in France, the wind gusting down from the Alps to the Mediterranean. When my father recovered, I would take him birding in the Alpilles and the Camargue. We'd eat bouillabaisse and daube de boeuf and clafoutis, and he would drink panachés, his preferred drink when he studied in Paris in the 1950s. We'd drive to Montaigne's castle near Bordeaux so my father could once again visit the tower library where Montaigne, his hero, wrote *Essais*. Together, we'd read the inscriptions on the wooden ceiling beams, including one that was perhaps my father's favorite: *Summum nec metuas diem, nec optes* (Neither be afraid of your last day nor desire it). I told him once that I would be sad forever when he died. "Oh no, don't be!" he said with a laugh. As a physician and a philosopher, he didn't fear death. If anything, he feared reaching the end of his life not having lived it.

## TRAVELING IN BARDO

My father's head was turned to the side, as if he were reorienting toward the horizon, already beginning his onward journey. I asked for a few moments alone with him because there were things I needed to say. I told him how much I loved him, how grateful I was for everything he had done for me and taught me. I thanked him for waiting for me to arrive from Tokyo and told him how much we wanted him to stay. But if he needed to go, we would understand.

My sisters and my father's friend returned to the room. Together, we watched the peaks and valleys on the monitor. Reassured by the regular rise and fall of the glowing line, I imagined my father's heart beating inside his broad chest, the great heart that had beat hour after hour, day after day—for him, for me, for us all—over eight decades. Then, impossibly, the valleys grew wider and wider, the beeps farther apart, and my father's heart stopped. I stared at the flat line, listening with horror to the interminable beeping sound. Just like that, at 2:19 p.m. on a sunny California afternoon, my father's life came to an end.

～

In Tokyo, there's a mood of impending absence, reminders everywhere that we can die at any moment and now is the time to live.

I'd never encountered cicadas before moving to Japan and was startled to hear their shrill, lively song burst forth in summer, when they emerge after years underground. I was even more surprised to learn that they vanish within a month or so. As Bashō writes,

> Nothing in the cry
> of cicadas suggests they
> are about to die

The cicadas shed their outer shell during their brief life aboveground; their exoskeletons can be seen attached to branches and leaves, as if to put you on notice that at any moment, you might leave your body.

Every day at five o'clock, the Japanese folk song "Yūyake koyake" (The Red Glow of Sunset) plays from loudspeakers in my neighborhood, summoning children home to their mothers:

> The sky glows as the sun sinks to the horizon,
> The bell at the mountain temple rings,
> Let's hold hands and all go home,
> Let's go home together with the crows...

Hauntingly wistful, especially at dusk in fall and winter, the song plays for about thirty seconds and then stops abruptly, mid-melody, as if to underscore contingency and the ever-present possibility of sudden endings. This feeling is intensified by the song's other purpose: It's a daily test of the nationwide broadcast system that stands ready to warn of emergencies like an industrial mishap, a missile attack by North Korea, a natural disaster.

Situated along the Ring of Fire, a 25,000-mile belt of seismic activity that stretches from Antarctica to the Aleutian Islands to the Andes, Japan has been subject to floods and tornadoes and conflagrations, volcanic eruptions and earthquakes, since ancient times. In his long poem *Hōjōki: A Hermit's Hut as Metaphor*, twelfth-century Buddhist monk Kamo no Chōmei writes of natural disasters in the capital city of Kyoto: a "great whirlwind" like "the winds of hell" in which "countless people lost their lives in the scramble to save their homes"; a fire in which people "were swallowed by flames, / [p]erishing immediately"; an earthquake when "those who stayed inside, / ... were crushed by their homes," and "those who tried to run, / ... were swallowed by the earth."

Now, as then, earthquakes are never far from people's minds, since hundreds occur in Japan every year. Most are small, perhaps causing the dishes to rattle or a book to fall from the shelf. But you never know if the shaking will escalate, especially because the next major earthquake isn't a matter of if, but when.

The last big temblor was on March 11, 2011, a clear day with an early spring chill in the air. I was at work when the building started to shake, and as the shaking grew stronger, I ran outside with my colleagues. The quake was magnitude 9.0, the largest ever recorded in Japan, with the epicenter about 200 miles northeast of Tokyo. Public transportation came to a halt, so I walked for three hours to get home, stopping with crowds of people to watch huge screens that showed tsunami waves—some close to 130 feet—thundering inland in prefectures to the north, engulfing towns and farmland. The quake devastated the country's eastern coast and triggered a nuclear meltdown at the Fukushima Daiichi Nuclear Power Plant.

Nearly 20,000 people died, and thousands more were injured or went missing. Many perished when they tried to return home to retrieve photos, desperate to preserve the family albums for the sake of their ancestors and their children. In a project called "Salvage Memory," the Japan Self-Defense Forces and volunteers recovered 750,000 photos from the mud and debris and scanned them into a searchable database. The images are achingly ordinary: a couple having dinner, a girl blowing out candles on a birthday cake, a student in uniform on the first day of school.

A magnitude 7.6 earthquake occurred on New Year's Day 2024 as I was writing this book. "Stop watching the news! Run for high ground!" TV announcers shouted after a tsunami warning was issued. Over 200 people died in the quake, many crushed in their homes while eating celebratory meals on the country's biggest holiday, and tens of thousands took refuge in evacuation shelters. The epicenter was at the tip of the Noto Peninsula on the Sea of Japan, miles from Tokyo, but our house swayed, and birds shrieked in the trees as the ground shook.

Not long before, I'd taken a driving trip with my husband and son around the peninsula. Subject to frequent tremors and in decline because of the migration of young people to the cities, industries such as fishing suffering from a labor shortage, and changes in global markets, the area was one of the places most evocative of uncertainty and imminent absence that I've ever been. As we traveled along mostly empty roads, we passed deserted restaurants, boarded-up karaoke bars, villages that seemed to have only elderly residents.

We stayed for a night in Wajima, a once-busy seaport. Exploring the cavernous, sparsely occupied hotel, we came upon dim, high-ceilinged banquet rooms with musty, faded curtains and dozens of chairs stacked upside down on tables. After a dinner of sashimi at one of the few restaurants in town that were open, we returned to our room and put out the futons on the threadbare *tatami* floor. David and Henry fell asleep, but I lay awake listening to the wind whistle through the eaves and watching a lone squid boat edge toward the horizon in the evening blue.

## WE MIGHT DIE TONIGHT

It's easy to forget that we might die tonight, but it's less easy in Japan. There's the capriciousness of nature, along with philosophies that imbue daily life with a sense of transitoriness, such as *mono no aware* (awareness of ephemeral beauty) and *wabi-sabi* (appreciation of aging and imperfection). Living in this kind of environment, I'm continually reminded that the things and people we love, and we ourselves, can vanish at any moment.

⁓

As we become aware of the unpredictability of our existence, we can evolve. One way to work toward awakening is by thinking about whether we're living in alignment with our authentic self. *The Tibetan Book of the Dead* exalts "the radiance of thine own true nature" as "subtle, sparkling, bright, dazzling, glorious, and radiantly awesome, in appearance like a mirage moving across a landscape in spring-time." We're told to "be not daunted…, nor terrified, nor awed" by this brilliant light; reassured that it's possible to go toward it and the time is now. On the misty morning that I visited Bhutia Busty monastery and learned more about the bardo principles, the lama talked with me about this, saying, "Most important is to spend a good human life. You get your precious body, but then"—he snapped his fingers—"it's gone. Do it now." If we don't go toward the light and embrace our path, he added, we can end up in one of the hell realms, and "it takes a pretty long time to get out."

*Be yourself.* It sounds simple, doesn't it? But we care too much about what others think, and when our last day is upon us, we wonder why we cared so much and wish we hadn't. In an interview for my series about bardo, writer Gish Jen told me how she recognized her true self when she was at the Stanford Graduate School of Business. "I went to a funeral for the first time," Jen said, "and realized, 'Oh, my god! We're all going to die!' I was going to die, and if I didn't try to become a writer, I would lie on my deathbed asking myself, 'Why did I not try to become a writer?' You can't lie on your deathbed with regret of that order. At the same time, I was the daughter of immigrants, and nice Chinese girls did not just drop out of graduate school." Much to her parents' dismay (they didn't speak to her for over a year), she left business school and entered the writing program at the University of Iowa.

The consciousness of her own mortality that struck Jen at the funeral has never left her. She said, "For every book, I ask myself, 'If it's only [possible] to write one more book, would this be it?'" Witnessing death, or understanding that it will assuredly arrive, can lead us to ask ourselves questions like this as we make decisions related to career, marriage, parenthood. Think for a moment about what some of your questions might be: *If I only have one more year to...*, *If there's only one more chance to...*

A tulip is a tulip, a willow is a willow. Tigers are tigers and butterflies are butterflies. Tulips and willows, tigers and butterflies, don't lose sight of what they are and end up being something else. (*I ended up a daffodil when I'm really a tulip! How did I turn into an aardvark when I'm actually a tiger?*) The capacity to live inauthentically is, unfortunately, all too human. We can become alienated from ourselves, often without realizing it.

This started for me when I was young. Like most girls, I strove to look pretty and be nice, hamstrung by society's messaging; by my mother's worry that I was a bold troublemaker; and by my father's Pygmalionish impulse to instruct, an occupational hazard for him as a psychiatrist. My father monitored my tone of voice and the way I smiled, my gestures and word choice. He cautioned me against being a people-pleaser—one of his most scathing indictments—even as I sought to please him. In a book of cartoons on his coffee table there was a drawing of Hamlet trying to figure out who, and whether, to be. Face contorted with effort and despair, the Prince of Denmark scrutinized lines and angles and mathematical equations scrawled on the ground (he was "pretzeled up," my father said)—that was how I felt.

I saw early on that boys who showed their real selves were determined, confident go-getters, but girls who did were stubborn, selfish know-it-alls. Fearful of being judged, I hovered on the sidelines instead of diving into things. I struggled to distinguish between unhealthy and healthy desire, between wanting to be a blue-eyed blonde and longing to be myself rather than who others wanted me to be. I thought about what bliss it would be to break free, but I never considered suicide—what I wanted to kill was my false self. Desperate for release, I had a recurring dream in which I lifted off from the ground at will and soared over cities and fields and forests to the open sea.

I sometimes sensed my genuine nature, like on winter days when I skated at the town pond with my friend Kathleen. We were faster than all the other skaters, driven by the unchecked joy of sprinting across the ice. There were kids who fell through into the dark water, broke arms and legs, but we never did. All these years later, I can still feel the cold air and the sun on my face, smell the damp earth and woodsmoke, see the bare trees silhouetted against the clouds sailing past, hear our shouts and laughter. I remember the electrifying power that coursed through me when, in and of the world instead of holding back, I felt my core self and my public persona click into alignment.

Only when I moved to Japan did I experience more lasting harmony between my inner and outer selves. *The Tibetan Book of the Dead* says that to achieve this, we must recognize the "habitual propensities" that make us flee the "radiance of [our] own true nature," ways of thinking and acting we've grown accustomed to that bind us to an inauthentic identity. One such propensity for me was my belief that pleasing others was an incontrovertible good. But safe in my teahouse, the wide Pacific between me and the Greek chorus I'd grown up with, I felt this notion lose its grip. I imagined I was like Flaubert after he left his native France for Egypt, a place where, he said, he could dream and feel at home. *Who do you think you are?* The meaning of the question that haunted me in girlhood became an invitation to exploration instead of self-censure. When I settled in Tokyo, a friend told me that the plant I'd given her years earlier, that had survived but never thrived, had at last bloomed.

A striking, and heartening, aspect of authenticity is that it's not about *creating* your essential self. In Buddhist belief, that self is like the wide blue sky, sometimes obscured by clouds but already and always existing. It becomes visible as we let go of unskillful ways of being, as we shed false personas and allow who we are to emerge.

There are questions we can keep in mind that help us do this: If you found out you were going to die soon, what are some things (like others' approval) that you would stop caring about? What would make you feel free? This kind of reflection can awaken us to the radiance of our true nature, an opportunity that, like the clear sky, is ever present.

Living with the awareness that we might die tonight includes showing up for the people we love. Think about your parents, your children, a close friend—What would you do with or for them if you knew there wouldn't be time later? It might be calling your father once a week instead of every few months, setting aside an afternoon for your mother to show you how to make her special quiche, taking more outings with your children, going on a long-postponed holiday with a friend. What would you regret not having done if this were your last moment, or that person's last moment?

I thought a lot about this when, some years ago, my mother started asking me to travel with her to Dharamsala, home-in-exile of the Dalai Lama, and to her hometown of Darjeeling. I decided I'd do it later—I was busy with teaching and writing and the children, and besides, trips with my mother were like those games you play where your parents warn you to stop because somebody's going to get hurt. But working in my study one evening, moonlight glazing the tile roofs of the neighboring houses, I changed my mind. I was writing a bardo-themed novel about the struggle between mother and daughter, and the love that binds them, and I could almost hear the clock ticking. My mother would soon be eighty, and now that she was growing old, maybe she wanted to make a pilgrimage back home to reconnect with her roots. I didn't want to regret not having helped her do that.

# WE MIGHT DIE TONIGHT

And so we set off for India. Arriving in Dharamsala, we toured the town, gorging ourselves on momo dumplings and *thukpa* noodle soup, shopping for jewelry and embroidered shawls, and attending a public audience with the Karmapa, head of one of Tibet's oldest lines of reincarnate lamas. As I'd expected, we had our differences, but what struck me most were the startling reminders of the precariousness of life. Short of breath one afternoon as we walked about, my mother said, "I'm very aware of my mortality." On the stairs to our hotel near the Dalai Lama's temple and residence, she fell. Her fingers felt birdlike and fragile as I helped her to her feet, and there was a rapidly swelling bruise on her forehead. Saddened that she must suffer the indignities of aging, that her body might not be up to the challenge of the trip she'd longed to make, I took her arm and we continued climbing.

At night, my mother lay in bed reading Jhumpa Lahiri's *Unaccustomed Earth*, which she'd bought when we arrived. A collection of stories about Indian American immigrants, their American children, and the search for identity and belonging, the book takes its title from what Nathaniel Hawthorne wrote in his preface to *The Scarlet Letter*: "Human nature will not flourish, any more than a potato, if it be planted and replanted, for too long a series of generations, in the same worn-out soil." His children, Hawthorne hoped, would "strike their roots into unaccustomed earth." By settling in America, my mother had found unaccustomed earth and flourished, but at what price? Now, back in the country where she was born—almost sixty years after she took off for New York, sleeping close to the Dalai Lama—did she feel she'd lost, or sacrificed, too much?

After a few days in Dharamsala, we continued on to Darjeeling, and our week there shed light on these questions. My mother was delighted to once more visit her old haunts, including the Gymkhana Club, where she used to roller skate and play ping-pong, and Glenary's, where she'd noshed on tea and pastries with her school chums. She caught up with the shopkeepers, some of whom had taken over from their parents and had known her since she was small, cajoling them into giving her good prices and little gifts. I wondered if she was feeling nostalgic for her girlhood; this was clarified one day over drinks in the Windamere sitting room as we chatted with hotel guests, who were eager to hear my mother's story.

"I left at nineteen and never came back," my mother said. "I was a renegade."

"Do you miss Darjeeling?" someone asked.

She laughed. "Not in the least!"

Driven by her desire to escape an environment that she'd found limiting, my mother had never been burdened by the exile's longing for home. The ease she felt on this peaceful evening, conversing leisurely as the smell of coal drifted from the fire and ponies clip-clopped past in the street below, could only have been earned through going away and returning as both insider and visitor.

The day before we left, my mother had a special *puja* prayer service performed at the house for my grandmother, who'd been dead four years. In spite of their struggles, my mother's love and sense of duty had never wavered. When she came to America, she was relieved to cast aside the Buddhist ceremonies she'd grown up with, what she called "all that hocus pocus," but her filial responsibility extended to making sure the rituals that had mattered so much to my grandmother were carried out.

On that trip, my mother went home as a Tibetan and as a daughter. Perhaps in asking me to accompany her, she had understood—thanks to her Buddhist upbringing and her training as a physician—what I at first couldn't grasp: The moment for the journey was now, because things could change without warning. In the future to come, she would barely survive a ruptured aneurysm and then begin a slow descent into dementia. So, after all, there would not have been time later.

That would be our last trip together to India, just the two of us.

Once when I was visiting my grandmother, she handed me a notebook and said, "You can use this to write my biography." Since she was living a long and healthy life, I thought there would be plenty of time for this project down the road, but she was so eager that I began recording her recollections in writing and on tape. Now that she's gone, I'm grateful that I did this before it was too late.

My grandmother had a message for her children, grandchildren, great-grandchildren, and the generations to follow. "I wish you all the best of luck," she said. "May you prosper and do well. I bless you with all my prayers, and always I pray for your happiness and prosperity. It is a wonderful life." Her joie de vivre was rooted in her understanding that the way to find meaning in a world where at any moment we—and everything we love—can cease to exist, is to live your life as fully as possible. Here are some of her principles:

### BE TRUE TO YOURSELF

When my grandmother was living in Lhasa with her father, she received a marriage proposal. Her father said, "There's a cabinet minister's son who wants to get married to you. Are you interested?" My grandmother replied, "Father, I wouldn't like to. I'm afraid not." If you married a nobleman, she told me, "*every* day you had to wear that Tibetan headdress and lots of jewelry, lean forward all the time. Very heavy. I hated it. You had to only live like a lady and play mah jong. I would have died of boredom. And the traditional wives have to respect the husbands with the hands pressed together, worship the he-man."

## DON'T WASTE TIME WORRYING

In her study, my grandmother kept a *Losar* New Year's greeting card from the Office of the Dalai Lama that said,

> If there is a remedy,
> Why be unhappy about it?
> If there is no remedy,
> What is the use of being unhappy about it?
> *Shantideva (8th-century Indian Scholar and Saint)*

## HAVE FUN

My grandmother worked hard all her life, but she knew how to have a good time. She was an ace pontoon player and the first one out on the dance floor. She and my grandfather threw epic parties at the house, whiskey and pink gin flowing, rumba and cha cha and jazz playing on the phonograph, everyone dancing the Tibetan Charleston. And she never lost her childlike nature: In one of our old family movies, my mother and her four siblings and their six cousins are having a snowball fight. In the middle of the hubbub is my grandmother, winding up again and again to hurl snowballs, laughing merrily.

## PRACTICE ACCEPTANCE

"Life is not a bed of roses, everything does not go the way we want," my grandmother often said. "We Buddhists believe it's a great sin not to be satisfied with your life." When my mother married in America and my grandfather took it especially hard, my grandmother told him, "*What* sense does it make? What good is going to come by you feeling sad and regretting? This is the way things were to be."

## TAKE YOUR CHANCES AS THEY COME

At a Calcutta airfield in the 1930s, my grandparents were among the first to fly on the Tiger Moth biplane. "The old Tibetan gentleman who was with us, he wouldn't try it!" my grandmother told me. "He said, 'Thank you, I don't want to get killed.' But your grandfather and I each took a spin because we thought it was a pity not to give it a go!"

I see my grandmother climbing in behind the pilot in her long *chuba* dress, wearing the dark movie-star sunglasses she favored. I smell the fuel, the grass burning in the heat, the pilot's coconut hair oil and my grandmother's Elizabeth Arden perfume. The air grows cool as the plane ascends high over the patchwork of green and brown fields surrounding the sprawl of the city, the Hooghly River snaking down toward the Bay of Bengal. The crowd of onlookers recedes and there's only the rushing of the wind, the endless expanse of the Indian sky on a clear day, of life stretching ahead in all its happiness and uncertainty.

~

In his preface to the second edition of *The Tibetan Book of the Dead*, Evans-Wentz expressed the hope that "the Occident might reformulate and practise an Art of Dying, and, also, an Art of Living." Practicing the art of living means not wasting the limited amount of time that we have. Most of us don't want to squander our days, but in the whirl of ordinary life this can be easy to forget.

One way that we can keep it in mind is with the help of *memento mori*, reminders that we must die, which are also *memento vivere*, reminders that we must live. They're seen in seventeenth-century Dutch paintings in the form of clocks, broken dishes, faded blooms, overripe fruit, a page torn from a calendar, and in contemporary works like Jean-Michel Basquiat's skull paintings and Damien Hirst's cast of a human skull covered with thousands of diamonds. They also include celebrations such as Día de los Muertos in Mexico, when altars with flowers and food are set up to honor the dead as they return for a visit; the Japanese *Obon* festival, when *chōchin* lanterns are lit and dances are performed to welcome back the ancestors; and Tibetan sky burials and funerals. Rousing us from the dream of immortality, they embolden us to live now.

What is one of your memento mori / memento vivere? Is it an object? A song? A ritual? In Tokyo, crows are everywhere—perched on stone walls and grave markers, telephone lines and rooftops—and their caw-cawing always sounds to me like exhortations toward an enlightened life, as if they're saying, "Live, live, live!" They make me think of fifteenth-century poet and Zen master Ikkyū Sōjun, who achieved *satori* (saw the nature of reality) when he was meditating in a boat on Lake Biwa, near Kyoto, and heard a crow call. They remind me that crows are messengers of Yama, Lord of Death and symbol of impermanence, and are believed to be incarnations of Mahakala, a many-armed, flame-encircled, wrathful deity who defends the dharma, the teachings of the Buddha. Mahakala is terrifying, but, as one of the lamas at my grandmother's funeral explained, "in a good way," reminding us to live with authenticity and passion.

My memento mori / memento vivere include my great-grandfather's photograph of the sky burial outside Lhasa, Mac's bones in the brocade-covered urn in the living room, and my well-worn copy of *The Tibetan Book of the Dead*. There's also a turquoise pendant my mother gave me before I left for college, given to her by my grandfather when she left for medical school in America. It reminds me of the day I dropped my daughter off at college, of the blue summer sky as I watched her walk away from me toward the brick buildings, wearing the shorts and eyelet T-shirt she'd picked out the week before when we went shopping in Tokyo, the gladiator sandals I bought her when I was in Paris teaching a writing workshop. She glided over the grass—a trick of the light and shadow? The chapel bells struck five and the carillon played, its plangent, lovely notes ringing out in the golden air, drawing the past to a close and heralding the future. By the time the music finished, my daughter had disappeared and I was alone in the quiet afternoon.

A memento mori / memento vivere can also be a book, like Montaigne's *Essais*, or a poem, perhaps Jane Kenyon's "Otherwise," which she wrote after being diagnosed with leukemia. She reflects on an ordinary day spent walking the dog, writing, making love, looking forward to the same kind of day tomorrow, even as she's aware that the day will come when things are "otherwise."

Another kind of memento mori / memento vivere is an image of a painting, such as Frida Kahlo's *Viva la Vida*, an exuberant statement of delight and love of life in the face of decay and vanishing. During a college semester abroad in Mexico City, I visited Kahlo's house, La Casa Azul, where she painted *Viva la Vida* as she neared death in the summer of 1954. She had suffered greatly: When she was a child, she contracted polio, and at eighteen, she was in a streetcar accident that consigned her to dozens of surgeries and debilitating pain throughout her life. She illustrated her agony in self-portraits that showed her bleeding, with internal organs exposed and nails and arrows piercing her face and body.

At La Casa Azul, I gazed at *Viva la Vida* and imagined Kahlo seated in the wheelchair at the wooden easel in her studio, composing the painting as the July rains cascaded down the tall windows overlooking the jacarandas and bougainvillea in the courtyard garden. Ill with pneumonia, she knew the end was approaching as she completed this final work, which depicts watermelons in a landscape of earth and sky, some split open and ripe with seeds. "Sliced and chopped, the pieces of fruit acknowledge the imminence of death," Hayden Herrera tells us in *Frida*, her biography of Kahlo, "but their luscious red flesh celebrates the fullness of life." On one of the watermelons, Kahlo wrote "VIVA LA VIDA": *Long live life.*

The glory and challenge of being human is that we can make as much or as little of our days on this earth as we choose. We may hold life at arm's length because we're attached to ways of being that don't serve us; we may put off throwing ourselves at the feet of Miss X because we think we can do it later. Now is the time to see that one day, things will be otherwise for you and for me, for every one of us; not only is our time finite, but we don't know how much time we have. In the face of this unequivocal truth, the only way to find true happiness is by plunging into life.

# 7.
# HAIL-STORMS AND WHIRLWINDS OF ICY BLASTS

*A Bardo Journey*

O nobly-born, although one liketh it not,... one feeleth compelled involuntarily to go on;... noises and snow and rain and terrifying hail-storms and whirlwinds of icy blasts occurring, there will arise the thought of fleeing from them.

—*The Tibetan Book of the Dead*

Leis go brown, tectonic plates shift, deep currents move, islands vanish, rooms get forgotten.

—Joan Didion
*The Year of Magical Thinking*

On September 13, 2010, I lay in a Tokyo hospital, my joints aching and my skin burning hot. Only a faint glow of daylight penetrated the privacy curtain. The routine of temperature-taking, breakfast, and doctors' rounds hadn't started yet, so the room was silent except for the beeping of monitors and an occasional rattling snore from the elderly woman in the next bed.

Sunk in that dimness, and staring up at the ceiling, I remembered my grandmother's account of the morning in 1912 when her father was caught in an avalanche after helping the Dalai Lama return to Tibet from exile in India. I imagined that winter day: the dragon blue Himalayan sky; the sun glittering on the ice-encrusted pines; the groaning of the ponies and pack animals, their musky smell; the labored breathing of the trapped men as panic rose in their throats. I saw my great-grandfather struggling in his twilit bardo to pull out his rosary and reach for the air, listened as he prayed to his beloved Guru Rinpoche; I heard the shouts of the men aboveground as they ran over to help.

I'd been admitted to the hospital a week earlier, suffering from a severe headache and nausea, an unremitting fever of 103, and violent chills. David and I had been on summer holiday with our children in Indonesia, and my doctors thought I might have contracted dengue fever or malaria. None of my symptoms had abated, and every day new ones were appearing: a jaundiced tinge to my skin, tiny red petechiae dots on my hands from subdermal bleeding, a pebbly rash on my knees, photophobia. The pain in my joints was so excruciating that I now understood why dengue, if that's what I had, was known as "breakbone fever."

The week had passed in a blur of pain and confusion as my symptoms worsened and my doctors tried to figure out what was wrong. New words entered my Japanese vocabulary: *samuke* (chill), *darui* (extreme lassitude), *enshō* (inflammation), *tenteki* (IV). I underwent head CT scans and full-body CT scans; regular MRIs and contrast-enhanced MRIs; X-rays and echocardiograms; agglutination and nephelometry tests; SGOT and SGPT liver function tests; tests for lupus, Sjögren's syndrome, and rheumatoid arthritis. The CRP (C-reactive protein) test, an indicator of inflammation in the body, showed that my level was 16 instead of less than 1. Too weak to walk, I was taken for the tests in a wheelchair.

On September 15, my tenth day in the hospital, one of the doctors, Dr. Kondo, rushed in and, flinging his arms wide like an umpire, announced, "Final diagnosis! Endocarditis." He spoke fast, yet unbearably slowly: Endocarditis was a rare, life-threatening infection of the endocardium, or heart lining. Bacteria got into the bloodstream, attached to the endocardium—often in a heart valve—and formed a mass, or vegetation. The vegetation in my mitral valve had proliferated to 20.3 millimeters, so large it would have begun forming four to six weeks earlier.

"It is lucky," Dr. Kondo said, "that you have not experienced a heart attack." I'd need to stay for four more weeks to receive intravenous ceftriaxone and ciprofloxacin, antibiotics that might or might not work.

*That might or might not work.* I contracted into a knot of fear and bewilderment.

After Dr. Kondo left, I hobbled with my IV stand to the hallway computer to google endocarditis. The smooth, cool feel of the keys under my fingertips calmed me, as always. Now I'd be able to see the whole picture. I would put my thoughts in order and formulate a plan. But as the information flashed onto the screen, my mind grew charged and staticky, my breathing ragged: *Complications include congestive heart failure, severe organ damage, intracranial hemorrhage, stroke, neurological failure. Difficult to cure. Significant mortality.*

⁓

Serious illness throws us into a liminal state, suspending our usual reality and launching us on a terrifying bardo journey. When I fell ill with endocarditis, I was no longer learning the *Tibetan Book of the Dead* principles in lovely monasteries or my grandmother's cozy living room or my peaceful study. Instead, I was hurtling through a dark tunnel of physical, emotional, and psychological pain, forced to confront impermanence in the most elemental, unrelenting way.

## TRAVELING IN BARDO

Have you ever felt not quite yourself, like you're mysteriously out of sync with your usual rhythms? My ordeal started with this kind of feeling—which I experienced as intimations of impermanence—when we were in Indonesia. It was Ramadan, and every morning, I lay sleepless, listening to the muezzin sing the call to prayer in the still, blue dawn. Like it was my last hour, regret over matters large and small flooded me: hurtful things I'd said or done, actual and imagined slights, lost opportunities.

My unease continued after we flew home to Tokyo from Jakarta, especially one evening toward the end of August. Our neighborhood was quiet, as if resting after the sweltering heat of the day. We'd opened the windows, and a twilight breeze brought in the odor of damp earth from the garden, along with laughter from a neighbor's TV, the occasional *ting* of a glass wind chime, and the plaintive song of the gyoza dumpling vendor as he wound through the streets.

An evening like so many others, but glancing up from the newspaper, I was transfixed. David sat at the dining table in a tattered Cape Cod T-shirt and khaki shorts, working on his computer. Fourteen-year-old Sophia was sprawled on the floor doing geometry problems and eating *mikan* tangerines; twelve-year-old Henry sat cross-legged on the sofa, writing out Japanese *kanji* characters. Mac slumbered under the table next to his bone, paws twitching as he dreamed his doggie dreams.

We usually don't think much about death when we're in the midst of our beautiful lives. But that evening, it was as if I could hear the words of the Buddha in the *Diamond Sutra*, an ancient scripture whose wisdom slices through our illusions with the sharpness of a diamond:

> Thus shall ye think of all this fleeting world:
> A star at dawn, a bubble in a stream,
> A flash of lightning in a summer cloud,
> A flickering lamp, a phantom, and a dream.

Before long, the life I loved would fade away. Sophia would leave for college and Henry would go soon afterward. Not much later, Mac would be dead! I saw David and myself retiring from our universities and growing old, our house being torn down. All the things that hadn't happened yet but inevitably would.

My unsettling feelings persisted for a week—perhaps caused by the vegetation that, unbeknownst to me, was proliferating in my heart valve—until I woke up one morning very sick and landed in the ER.

Over the days to come, my journey would resonate eerily with the voyage through bardo described in *The Tibetan Book of the Dead*. Soon after I was admitted to the hospital, the head doctor, Dr. Ando, stopped by and gazed at me with an expression both intrigued and perplexed, as if he were wondering how this extremely ill American woman had come to be under his care.

"Have you... been in Japan for quite a long time?" he asked.

When I told him I'd lived in Tokyo for almost a quarter of a century, he looked surprised. When I said that I was a mother of two, a writer, and a literature professor, he looked astonished. I shared his amazement: In my diminished state, the person I'd described seemed like someone else. I'd taken leave of my full, rich life and was viewing it from afar, just as the dead person hovers in bardo, gazing back at the existence to which she can never return.

Nights, I lay in bed listening to sirens shriek in the labyrinthine streets of the city and the elderly woman next to me rave in her sleep, calling out "Iya da!" *It's not okay!* I longed for heavy, narcotic slumber—for an escape, however brief, from the terrifying reality I'd fallen into—but if I managed to drift off, it was into a realm of nightmares. I was trapped inside a shack in the hottest desert in the world, dust blowing through gaps between the floorboards, everything shriveled, brown, desiccated. Driving on a dark, winding road in torrential rain, I lost control of the car and plunged off the edge. I dreamed that my ID had been stolen and wild dogs were attacking me.

I felt like I was wandering in the bardoscape depicted in *The Tibetan Book of the Dead*, a place where you hear "songs like wailings" and are enveloped in "thick awesome darkness"; you experience "apparitional illusions... of being pursued by various terrible beasts of prey." Once, I shot up in bed and called to David, who was dozing in the chair next to me, but he didn't wake. *This is the after-death bardo*, I thought. I was in the stage of the journey where, not yet realizing we are dead, we call out to our loved ones but they cannot hear us.

I prayed that my luck would turn, but I must have sensed that I was traveling further into bardo, as I dreamed one night that I was flying deeper and deeper into a rugged, primeval valley, the trees shrouded in mist.

Indeed, things got much worse. Two days into the antibiotic therapy, the vegetation in my mitral valve had shrunk almost 40 percent. David and I were overjoyed; at this rate, I'd probably even be discharged early. But Dr. Ando was standing motionless at the foot of the bed, frowning deeply. At first, I attributed this to Japanese reserve or professional caution, but the gravity of his expression made me shiver. "When the vegetation appears to have shrunk rapidly," he said, "one possibility is that parts of it have broken off and embolized into the circulation." The emboli might reach my kidneys, he went on, leading to renal failure. They might travel to my brain and obstruct a blood vessel, causing a stroke. Or they could block a coronary artery, resulting in a heart attack.

That night I hardly slept, tormented by the usual feverish nightmares and fear of the emboli that might be moving through my veins like time bombs. When dawn came at last, gray and dreary, I felt so grateful to be alive that the morning looked beautiful despite its melancholy.

Breakfast arrived, and as I took hold of the chopsticks, I realized I couldn't feel them against the tip of my ring finger. I tested it with my other hand; it was numb. There was also a shimmering at the edge of my field of vision, like heat rising from a road.

I was taken immediately for an emergency MRI and CT scan, and this is how it was discovered that a piece of the vegetation had lodged in the occipital lobe of my brain, causing a large abscess, or pocket of infection, to form. If the abscess cut off blood flow to the surrounding tissue, I could suffer paralysis, "irreversible cognitive impairment," or—Dr. Ando paused, searching for the right words— "even more critical complications."

I was started on IV glycerol to reduce the size of the abscess, but two days later a neurosurgeon on my team showed me and David an image from the MRI I'd had that morning and told us, "Quite a bit more enlargement has taken place." As they'd feared, this had led to infarction, or obstruction of the blood supply, resulting in the death of the surrounding tissue. I stared at the image: In the lower left quadrant of a ghostly ovoid, a black orb was expanding, destroying my brain.

I thanked the neurosurgeon and started back to bed in my wheelchair. The sound of David pressing the doctor with questions faded as I inched along the corridor, struggling to push down the horror and dread surging inside me. The big stuffed Snoopy and Hello Kitty on the counter of the nurses' station looked forlorn, as though they knew what little consolation they could offer in this outpost of misery.

When David returned to my room, he told me the doctors were considering drastic, last-ditch measures. They might try drilling a burr hole in my skull to drain the abscess. If this failed, the only hope might be a craniotomy, where they would remove a piece of my skull bone to expose and evacuate the abscess.

I'd always imagined that if a moment like this came for us, we'd say what we didn't say in our ordinary, busy lives: *There has only ever been you.* We had important things to tell each other, now.

But we fell silent, alone together in the beeping, hissing night.

During serious illness, it seems that the earth beneath us has given way and we're whirling through space. In Buddhism, this is groundlessness, the realization that the ground we believed was solid and unchanging can disintegrate in a moment. Now, a long-forgotten memory came back to me, of another time when I was spinning in the void. It was the late eighties, soon after David and I married, and we took a holiday to a volcanic island in Fiji. Every day it poured rain, turning the dirt roads to muddy rivers, so we spent our time diving. One morning we did a drift dive, the kind where you descend holding on to a rope until you get below the strongest part of the current, close to the ocean floor. But we let go too soon, and unable to see the bottom or the surface, were lost together in the endless blue.

During those dark, terrible weeks in the hospital, I fell into denial, yearning for my former existence like the dead man my grandmother had told me about who tried to reenter his corpse. Like the protagonist in *The Seven Moons of Maali Almeida*, who insists he must return to his old life because he has photos to share, I wanted to tell whoever was in charge of the strange world I now inhabited that, why, just fifteen minutes away was my home, the modern Japanese house David and I had designed together, with our Le Creuset cookware and the Tibetan rugs I'd inherited from my grandmother, the rooftop balcony where we enjoyed apéros with friends on summer evenings, the fireplace we gathered around when the weather grew cold. I needed to explain that I had classes to teach at my university, that it was time to attend parents' night at the high school where Sophia was starting as a freshman, and eat *dango* rice flour dumplings with Henry at his school's *otsukimi* autumn moon viewing celebration.

Again and again, I assured myself that there was no way I could die, because I was in the prime of life. I'd always felt sure that I was destined to live to one hundred like my grandmother, that I wouldn't die before my time (fortunately, I only learned after I recovered that my other grandmother, my father's mother, died from endocarditis when she was twenty-eight). At some point, though, I realized with chilling clarity that in the Tibetan way of looking at things, "before your time" had no meaning. When my grandmother died on that winter night in Darjeeling, the moon setting over the peaks of Kanchenjunga and dogs howling far below in the valleys, she wasn't sick. Her body had just wound down. "It was her time," explained one of the lamas who came to do the prayers from *The Tibetan Book of the Dead*—she had reached the end of her allotted lifespan.

"One day you may be king or queen," my grandmother often said, "but when that is finished, you must accept it." If this was the end for me, I wanted to embrace it with equanimity, but I refused to accept that I might die in my forties. *As long as we both shall live*, David and I had promised that August afternoon—our life together couldn't possibly be over. And I had to see our children graduate from college, go to their weddings, hold their babies.

I'd experienced moments when I could have died but didn't. At nine, I was chased through the woods by a knife-wielding man; at seventeen, I missed an oncoming car by inches as I sped around a curve, driving to my boyfriend's house on a bright California morning. Surely getting sick with endocarditis was just another one of these moments.

We never know what will happen in the bardo between birth and death, but this usually doesn't trouble us too much because we assume we'll be around for a long time. When the life we're accustomed to is suspended by illness, though, the uncertainty of existence is thrown into bewildering relief.

The confusion we feel is captured in *The Tibetan Book of the Dead*'s description of the "swoon" we find ourselves in after death. The text explains, "The deceased can see that the share of food is being set aside, that the body is being stripped of its garments, that the place of the sleeping-rug is being swept; can hear all the weeping and wailing of his friends and relatives, and, although he can see them and can hear them calling upon him, they cannot hear him calling upon them."

When we're ill, we experience profound not-knowing. It isn't the not-knowing of beginner's mind, when you're curious about the nature of sleep or where the rain comes from—when you ask, as Montaigne did, "Que sais-je?"

It's not-knowing rooted in fear.

Like the deceased as she watches her body being stripped and hears her friends and family call out to her, we wonder, *What is happening?* We flail about, desperate to gain control, aghast that we live in a universe where random things (like a heart valve infection) can strike us down.

## HAIL-STORMS AND WHIRLWINDS OF ICY BLASTS

I remember feeling this way as the pandemic tore us away from our everyday reality and thrust us into a state of suspension. There was so much we didn't know. Where did the SARS-CoV-2 virus come from? How did it spread? Would we or the people we loved fall ill or die? When would the pandemic end? *Would* it end? Conspiracy theories, fake news, and constantly changing restrictions baffled us; we felt growing dismay and panic as variants of the virus appeared, lockdowns were extended, and borders were closed. Even if we were sheltering in our customary environments, our houses and neighborhoods, the familiar became unfamiliar as we were cut off from the daily routines that made us feel secure.

Thinking back on the disorientation I felt during the pandemic and, nine years earlier, when I was ill, I'm reminded of how, as a girl, I used to wake up in the middle of the night and have no idea where I was. I could see the glowing numbers on my digital clock, floating, Dali-esque, in the darkness, and the outlines of my dresser and window, but I groped about my bedroom, wondering if I was awake or dreaming. I think this was a response to the emotional instability of my day-to-day existence, because I'd found that under the veneer of ordinary life, dreadful events could occur without warning or explanation. When I was ten, we moved from New Jersey to California, and I thought this would be a fresh start for my parents, who hadn't been getting along, and for us as a family. But soon after we arrived in the Bay Area, my father left. A while later, I noticed that my mother was meeting regularly with a Mr. B—. I searched for his name in the phone book, discovered he was a lawyer, and realized with horror that my parents were getting divorced.

When I grew up and set off into the world, I sought order. One reason I fell in love with Japan is that it's a country where you know what to expect. Trains leave on time and people follow the rules. Lost wallets are returned to the nearest police box with money and credit cards intact. When people leave the house, they say *ittekimasu* (I'm leaving and will come back safely); when they return home, they say *tadaima* (I'm home).

The clean, systematized neighborhood where I lived in my teahouse made me feel as if I'd stepped into *Madeline*, a story I adored when I was small because, I would later see, it was about how order (twelve little girls at a boarding school in Paris "left the house at half past nine, in two straight lines, in rain or shine") could be created and relished as a bulwark against the unexpected (Madeline's emergency appendectomy). In Japan, stability was elevated to an art of living, even though—or perhaps because—unpredictable events such as typhoons and earthquakes could occur at any time.

In Tokyo, ensconced in the well-ordered environment I'd longed for, I built my career, started a family, managed my finances, and took care of my health. But when I was diagnosed with endocarditis, these fortifications were swept away like a sandcastle at high tide. I was cast adrift in an ocean of not-knowing, where the things that make us feel anchored—going to the office, paying bills—had lost meaning, and events unfolded with the haphazard logic of dreams.

Like Gregor Samsa in Kafka's novella *The Metamorphosis*, who wakes up one morning to find he's been transformed into a giant insect yet still wants to go to work, I kept a log during my hospital stay, scratching out notes through the haze of my fever and pain. This made me feel that I had a future, one in which I'd be telling friends about my journey through bardo ("You'll never believe what happened next...") and writing about what I'd experienced. In a stylish pink journal, I jotted down the names of the tests I was being given, my temperature fluctuations, what I ate, what the doctors said (*Heart defect? A virus can trigger a collagen disease—scleroderma?*). Most of what I wrote was later incomprehensible, like the words you scrawl in the middle of the night to record your dream but can't decipher in the morning.

In the bardo of illness, we can get lost in projections of the mind, a kind of magical thinking. Keeping notes gave me the sense that I was taking charge, that I could influence the outcome of my illness. I'd had similar feelings when, struggling with anxiety and grief over my parents' divorce, I tried to deflect bad luck by doing things an even number of times: letting the phone ring, glancing over my shoulder, checking that the doors were locked. I made sure that nothing in my room was under stress—if a shirt was hanging on a hook, I took it down and laid it out on the bed so it could relax and breathe.

Our efforts to exert control when faced with the uncontrollable can be seen as both irrational and rational. In *The Year of Magical Thinking*, Didion writes about them as a type of "derangement." The first instance of this thinking after her husband dies occurs when she authorizes an autopsy, "[reasoning] that an autopsy could show that what had gone wrong was something simple," something the doctors would be able to fix. Viewed from another perspective, our attempts at control are what Polish anthropologist Bronisław Malinowski (whose work I learned about from David, my favorite anthropologist) considered a pragmatic way of coping with the anxiety aroused by dangerous situations in which the outcome is uncertain, as when fishermen in the Trobriand Islands recited spells for protection from storms and malign spirits on the high seas.

In the hospital, I entered a state of mind that was perhaps a combination of delirium and practicality, where reflecting on the old Tibetan methods of prognostication that my grandmother used to talk about calmed my fears. These methods included remedies produced by studying the shoulder blade of a sheep; *mo*, in which the lamas threw dice to receive guidance; and visits to oracles, like a woman my grandmother consulted at a monastery outside Lhasa in 1924 ("There was a nun, she had pockmarks, who used to go in a trance and foretell the future").

My grandmother herself was proficient in dream divination, as when she "pre-saw" her father's death in 1936. The day he was leaving for Kalimpong to campaign for the assembly seat, she went to him and whispered, "Father, I didn't have a very good dream. I don't think you should go."

"I can't help it, darling," he said, picking up his valise. "All the preparations are made, everyone is waiting for me. I have to go. I can't let the people down."

"If you do, Father, you will never come back." She'd seen his body being brought up to the sky, with a few drops of rain, but also sunshine. Everyone was saying, *Look! Look!*, and pointing as his body rose to heaven.

If my grandmother were still alive, I wondered, what would she prophesy for me?

―

Sometimes things that seem like wishful thinking turn out to be powerful ways of influencing what happens.

Casting about for encouragement as my chances of recovery grew increasingly dim, I recalled an obstacle-removing ceremony that was held in Darjeeling after my grandmother's death. The ritual had seemed fanciful to me—known as "Victory over Negative Forces," it was performed to remove the obstacles that the surviving relations can come up against after a loved one dies, impediments to their journey forward in the bardo from birth to death.

The ceremony took place at my grandmother's house on a cold morning a few days after the cremation. Clouds wreathed Kanchenjunga and the usual cacophony of car horns sounded from the lower part of town. The sharp scent of sacred burning juniper rose from a fire that had been lit in a corner of the garden. Together with relatives, I watched as long prayer flags tied to metal poles were erected for us on the hill above, where the household staff had arranged plates piled with sugar, curd, biscuits, *tsampa*, incense, butter, bananas, and apples as offerings for the deities. The guardian gods of the ten directions had been invited, along with those who'd been in meditation for thousands of years, so everything had to be just right.

The rinpoche who had carried out the death rituals for my grandmother was there to perform the ceremony. "The prayers will be especially effective," he assured us, "because a mantra chanted by one monk is equal to one hundred chanted by you." He lit a butter lamp and set it next to the prayer flags to "cut through the darkness of ignorance," then took his place at a low, brightly painted table near my grandmother's rose bushes. On the table was a mirror, representing clarity, and a peacock feather for dispersing purifying holy water from a copper vase.

Turning a two-headed *damaru* drum back and forth, ringing a bell symbolizing wisdom, and rotating a small brass double-scepter *dorje* representing compassion, Rinpoche intoned prayers for every wish to be fulfilled, every obstacle removed, every sentient being benefited. As he prayed, we threw handfuls of rice. Perched on the garden gate, my grandmother's three fat hens watched the proceedings, swiveling their heads back and forth in unison.

When the ceremony ended, the sun broke through the clouds, and a warm ray fell on the assembled group of family members bundled in wool shawls and down jackets. A breeze unfurled my prayer flag, revealing the invocations written in Tibetan script next to an illustration of a parasol, one of the lucky symbols, to ward off evil forces, accident, and disease. Even though I didn't see how the ceremony could work, this did all feel highly auspicious.

As if hearing my thoughts, Rinpoche looked at me and said, "You must have faith." There was no need, he explained, for deep-mind analysis, because the scriptures had already been dissected by scholars over the centuries. He added, "It is the same when you visit the gold dealer. You don't analyze the gold yourself. You trust that it is real."

Gesturing to the parasol on my prayer flag, he told me about an old woman who, when she walked around town, was seen to have a lucky white parasol atop her hat because she'd been doing a particular prayer with great faith. One day, someone told her she'd been making a small mistake in her recitation of the prayer. She began reciting the prayer correctly, her faith clouded by regret and self-doubt, and the parasol disappeared. Then a lama told her that the way she'd been doing the prayer all along was correct because her devotion had been pure.

I decided that I would try to have faith in the obstacle-removing ceremony. I didn't know how exactly to do this, but at least I could set aside my misgivings. Perhaps I'd be safeguarded from any troubles the future might bring even if I wasn't practicing properly.

In the hospital six years later, I remembered Rinpoche's words. I wondered if I'd generated enough faith (whatever this meant in my case) since that morning in my grandmother's garden. Because I'd at least been present at the ceremony, I took solace in something else Rinpoche had said: Even if your faith was insufficient, you could gain protection through the ritual, in the same way an ant could earn merit if it inadvertently circumambulated a temple on a piece of swirling dung in a flood.

I assumed that the obstacle I needed removed was endocarditis. But some time after I left the hospital, it occurred to me that perhaps the ceremony was less about subduing negative forces like illness than about defeating inner obstacles, like the ones Gautama faced when he sat under the bodhi tree to attain enlightenment and became the Buddha.

## HAIL-STORMS AND WHIRLWINDS OF ICY BLASTS

According to legend, Gautama was set upon by Māra, a demon who tried to keep him from awakening to the full range of human suffering and how we can break free of our pain into a new way of living. In *Buddha*, Karen Armstrong tells us that Māra threatened Gautama "with a massive army. Māra himself was mounted on an elephant that was 150 leagues high. He had sprouted 1,000 arms, each of which brandished a deadly weapon." Armstrong notes that Māra "represents what Jungian psychologists would, perhaps, call [our] shadow-side, all the unconscious elements within the psyche which fight against our liberation."

These unconscious elements include indolence and anger, craving and jealousy, discontent and pride. Could it be that my path through the bardo of illness had been impeded above all by my inner obstacles, like pining for the life I'd known?

Illness makes us suffer, I realized, but in the Buddhist view—and the bardo teachings—our unenlightened actions (whether of body, speech, or mind) are the fundamental cause of the pain we feel. Of course, physical recovery is our goal, but our greater aim should be to identify and change our unskillful behavior.

In this way, the "Victory over Negative Forces" ceremony helped me, allowing me to see the true nature of my obstacles and thus have a chance to overcome them.

Among the bardos that occur as we travel between birth and death, periods of illness offer great possibility for achieving freedom. Believed to provide a real-life experience of what awaits us in the after-death bardo, they're a chance not only to prepare for what will happen when we die but to live more fully now. If we survive, we can return from the beyond with visceral, firsthand knowledge forged in the crucible of illness and apply this wisdom in our day-to-day lives.

Becoming familiar with death in order to live well is addressed by Montaigne in his essay "To Philosophize Is to Learn How to Die." He writes, "There is nothing I inquire about more readily than how men have died: what did they say? How did they look? What expression did they have?... If I were a scribbler I would produce a compendium with commentaries of the various ways men have died. (Anyone who taught men how to die would teach them how to live.)"

Montaigne would have been eager to sit down with a type of Tibetan sojourner known as a *délok*. In *Magic and Mystery in Tibet*, Alexandra David-Néel describes these individuals as "the pseudo-dead," people who journey in after-death realms and then come back. Giving an account of the tradition in *The Tibetan Book of Living and Dying*, Sogyal Rinpoche says, "In Tibetan, *dé lok* means 'returned from death,' and...déloks are people who seemingly 'die' as a result of an illness, and find themselves traveling in the bardo.... After a week the délok is sent back to the body with a message from the Lord of Death for the living, urging them to spiritual practice and a beneficial way of life."

Traveling in the bardo of illness, coming face to face with death, gave me a new perspective on how we can live well in a world where nothing lasts forever. Having studied *The Tibetan Book of the Dead* for years, I thought I understood impermanence. But it wasn't until I journeyed through illness that I really *felt* it. In bardo, the teachings tell us, we're in search of a lost harmony. I'd always thought this meant we seek to restore our old life, but after I got sick, I saw it differently. It's about the harmony we lose when we forget that impermanence is the central truth of existence. Only when we remember that everything changes and ends can we achieve equilibrium.

This insight opened my eyes to impermanence as a chance to evolve. "Between stimulus and response there is a space," Austrian psychologist and Holocaust survivor Viktor Frankl is said to have observed. "In that space is our power to choose our response. In our response lies our growth and our freedom." Within the dark bardo of my illness, I glimpsed this power as I experienced the well-known phenomenon where we suddenly appreciate the beauty of ordinary existence. If I lived, I'd sew Halloween costumes for Sophia, Henry, and Mac, and we'd go trick-or-treating together. I'd plant rosemary in the garden and buy plump goldfish for the moss-covered stone basin. After writing all day, David and I would take walks, stopping to chat with friends and lingering over *aki-agari* autumn sake at an *izakaya* bar, Miles Davis's *Sketches of Spain* or *Birth of the Cool* playing in the background. I would cook for my family: Moroccan chicken with preserved lemons and olives, spinach and fenugreek with Indian paneer cheese, tagliatelle with hazelnuts and prosciutto.

In a conversation for my bardo interview series, author Dani Shapiro shared a story that reminded me of Frankl's words and the chance we have to find meaning within impermanence. When her husband was diagnosed with cancer, Shapiro drew inspiration from a Zen parable about a monk being chased by a tiger in the forest. She told me, "He gets to the edge of a cliff, and there's nothing to do but get eaten by the tiger or jump off the cliff. Except there's a vine, and the monk climbs onto the vine and sees a perfect ripe strawberry on the vine. He also sees a mouse that's crept out from a crevasse in the cliff. The mouse is munching on the vine, trying to get the strawberry, so the monk plucks the strawberry and eats it."

Suspended in bardo, the monk exercises his power—the power we all have—to choose his response: recognition of the opportunity available in the present moment (he relishes the ripe strawberry), even when we're in danger (the tiger poised above, ready to eat him) and made conscious that whatever time we have left in life is passing (the mouse nibbling on the vine). Hanging on the vine, unsure of whether her husband was going to make it, Shapiro developed "a feeling of deep knowledge, of walking with joy and gratitude and compassion and connection while carrying the awareness that life is so utterly fragile."

As I teetered between life and death, optimism and despair, my appreciation for everyday existence flowered into a more profound understanding of the bardo teachings. *The Tibetan Book of the Dead* advises us to take strength from our tutelary deity, be it the Buddha or Julia Child; now, mine was my great-grandfather. Reflecting on how he survived the avalanche, I saw that only by accepting the reality of his predicament was he able to take action and save himself. The bardo teachings urge us to accept "what is," but the still deeper wisdom lies in seeing that acknowledgment of our situation means action—of body, speech, and mind—rather than passivity. My great-grandfather's story (which I only now fully grasped, even though my grandmother had told it to me years before) helped me to sustain hope, to reach for the light from my own entombment in bardo.

Impermanence had engulfed me like the "terrifying hail-storms and whirlwinds of icy blasts" described in *The Tibetan Book of the Dead*, cutting me off from the world of the living. I could hear sounds—doctors' pagers, the rattle of the food cart—but saw only the white curtains around my bed, the white ceiling. Now, though, my thinking began to change. As I was wheeled down the hallway for another MRI, another CT scan, and caught sight through doorways of people suffering, of other lives and fears, I realized I only had to look around to be reassured that I wasn't at all alone, that I was navigating bardo alongside fellow travelers. It also dawned on me that falling ill means you *belong to* the world of the living. It means you're alive, because the dead don't get sick. It's a reminder, however painful, that we're human, that, as the Buddha taught, no one is immune to old age, sickness, and death.

This lesson is seen in a famous Buddhist allegory about a woman named Kisā Gotamī, who loses her young son and, anguished, begs the Buddha to return him to her. The Buddha agrees on the condition that she obtain a mustard seed from a home in her village where no one has been touched by death. She hurries from door to door but, unable to find any such household, understands the wisdom the Buddha wishes to share: Death is part of life.

What Gotamī discovers, and what we can learn from her travails, is not only that endings are inevitable, but also that we aren't alone in our heartache over them; that the law of impermanence unites rather than divides us. Freed from the grief caused by her unwillingness to accept the death of her child, uplifted by her new awareness of community, she dedicates herself to the teachings of the Buddha.

As a happily-ever-after story, this parable speaks to our desire for permanence, though not in the way we might imagine. Think about what "happily ever after" means to you. A lifelong partnership? Financial security? Our notions of contentment tend to revolve around freedom from loss and uncertainty, but more impermanence always awaits—and only when we recognize this can we find true happiness.

If I survived endocarditis, I thought, I'd live happily ever after, but within months of my recovery, the 3/11 earthquake devastated northeastern Japan and threw me and David into crisis. As powerful aftershocks rattled Tokyo and the damaged nuclear reactors melted down, we agonized over how to keep our family safe. The following year, my father died; a few months later, my mother suffered the brain bleed, coming so close to death that she saw loved ones who'd passed on beckoning to her from across a great abyss.

Impermanence is the way of the world. We can live happily ever after not by striving to fortify ourselves against change—an impossible goal that makes us miserable—but by accepting it as the essence of our beautiful, brief time here together.

My journey through the bardo of illness lasted six weeks.

When the abscess in my brain didn't respond to the glycerol, my doctors initiated high-dose dexamethasone steroid therapy to try to decrease the swelling. There was grave discussion of neurological complications and additional tests, of the danger of a stroke because the infection could weaken the blood vessels in my brain. "But the remaining three weeks of antibiotics must be completed," Dr. Ando said, "before we can evaluate what is required."

The days passed slowly. I slipped into a dream within a dream, drifted into a strangely calm bend in the dark river that had engulfed me. My periodic echocardiograms and CT scans showed decreasing mitral valve vegetation and brain swelling, and I started to feel a little less afraid. The abscess gradually scarred over and the dexamethasone was tapered.

On Wednesday, October 13, the antibiotic therapy at last came to an end. My temperature had returned to normal, and the headache, nausea, chills, joint pain, and visual disturbances had almost disappeared. The echocardiograms showed that the vegetation in my mitral valve had shrunk from 12.7 to 5 millimeters, a reduction that Dr. Ando believed was due to the ceftriaxone and ciprofloxacin. The brain abscess had decreased from 53 to 47 millimeters, and my blood cultures were clear of bacteria.

I was still at risk for a cerebral hemorrhage. If the infection had created weak spots—aneurysms—in the vessels of my brain and one of the aneurysms ruptured, blood would leak out, putting pressure on the brain tissue and compromising its oxygen supply. Hemorrhagic stroke was,

Dr. Ando said, "a catastrophic event" that often proved fatal or led to permanent brain damage.

They now needed to perform a cerebral angiogram to check for impaired vascular integrity. A catheter would be inserted into my groin and up into one of my neck arteries; contrast dye would then be sent through the catheter into the blood vessels of my brain. Watching X-ray images, the radiologist would study the movement of the dye through the blood vessels. If aneurysms were detected in the vessel walls, I'd have to stay in the hospital for two more weeks of antibiotic therapy—and, possibly, brain surgery—to try to repair the weakened areas.

I set my sights on making it to Henry's cross-country final that weekend. This was the first season he was competing, and I had missed all his races. I would, I decided, make it to that last one.

On Thursday afternoon, I was given a sedative and a local anesthetic, then wheeled to a brightly lit room. Two nurses lifted me onto an examining table, positioned me under a camera, and dimmed the lights. The radiologist chatted with me about the time he'd spent studying in Los Angeles as he observed the flow of the dye through my brain on a screen along the wall. A strap held my head in place, but I could see the image: a tangle of gossamer branches anchored by a thick trunk, like an Ansel Adams photo of a California oak in fog. "I'm from the San Francisco Bay Area," I told the doctor, and we talked about how beautiful the city looked from the Golden Gate Bridge, the lush green of the Marin Headlands above the blue Pacific.

Lulled by the sedative, the memories of where I grew up, the hum of the machinery, and the warmth of the room, I felt safe for the first time in many weeks and wished the exam would never end. But in only an hour, the doctor had finished.

"There's no problem," he said, patting me on the arm.

It was finally over.

The next morning, the October light golden on the gingko trees, David came to take me home. I could hardly believe that at long last I was walking out of the sterile, airless room where I'd been suspended in bardo, the room I might very well have left on a gurney, covered by a sheet.

Some nurses helped me and David pack, exclaiming, over and over, "Yokatta desu nee! Yoku ganbarimashita, nee!" *It's great, isn't it! You really hung in there!*

We gave them a tin of chocolate chip cookies the children had baked and a note they'd written, since they were at school:

> Thank you for taking care of our mother.
> Sincerely,
> Sophia and Henry

Dr. Ando and Dr. Kondo stopped in to say goodbye.

"Your case was very difficult," Dr. Ando said, his worry lines softened by a relieved smile. With typical Japanese humility, he added, "We learned a lot."

We thanked them again and again, but no words seemed adequate. How could you just say thank you and goodbye to the people who'd saved your life?

After more thank-yous and goodbyes and lots of bowing all around, David and I left. We dropped my things at home, where Mac launched himself at me, barking with joy, and then we went to lunch at a neighborhood trattoria.

At our table out on the terrace, David and I talked about everything that had happened, and he told me that when the brain embolism was discovered, the doctors felt I wasn't going to make it.

Yet here I was, I thought, immersed in the beauty of this impermanent world. All around me, the trees, the flowers, the signs, the cars pulsed in a dazzling array of greens, oranges, pinks, and reds; the sky was a brilliant turquoise. I'd lost ten pounds, my hair was thin, and I had track marks on my arms from the IV needles, but I was eating tomato-and-tuna pasta with my husband on a sunny fall day, my dog at my feet, people talking and laughing at the tables around us, the *ping* of a baseball bat sounding from a nearby field.

I'd returned from death, and would do all I could to practice what I'd discovered about how to live.

# 8.
# WE ARE THE ARTISTS OF OUR LIVES

The words and meanings [of this doctrine] should be committed to memory by every one;... There is no doubt as to its liberating.
—*The Tibetan Book of the Dead*

Continually he had to verify online that he was not a robot.... Confirm your humanity, was the request.
—Lorrie Moore
*I Am Homeless if This Is Not My Home*

On a fall afternoon in Darjeeling about twenty years ago, I went to see a local official who'd arranged a meeting for me with some monks. I was writing a novel related to bardo and had a few questions. "The monks have gone to the cave," the man announced when I arrived at his office. I told him I'd come back later in the week but he shook his head. The cave was in the south of India and the monks would be there until spring.

Continuing on my way, I came to Chowrasta, the town plaza. I turned onto the promenade circling the foot of prayer-flag-wreathed Observatory Hill, where my family used to celebrate *Losar* New Year, and where our ancestor Lama Rinzing Dorji Laden La founded the monastery. Somewhere on this hill, I recalled, was a cave that hermits had once used for meditation, and that was said to lead to sacred Buddhist caves in Tibet. As I walked along with tourists, elderly Tibetans counting their prayer beads, and people out for their daily constitutional, I wondered where exactly the hermit cave was. I thought about the monks who'd "gone to the cave" in the south and how they had entered a between-state that held the possibility of deeper insight.

In the Buddhist tradition, caves are thought to offer an opportunity for new understanding. Removed from daily life, they're quiet, simple spaces that invite reflection; time spent in a cave is a kind of bardo. My grandmother knew a rinpoche from Ghoom who vanished and was discovered to have gone to a high cave in Yatung, near Tibet, where he stayed for three years "getting power." ("People wondered who was feeding him, *who* was feeding him?" she said. "It was the yeti that was feeding him, on berries and all that.")

Gautama retreated to a cave near Bodh Gaya on his journey to becoming the Buddha, and in the eleventh and twelfth centuries the Tibetan spiritual master Milarepa sought enlightenment "in six well-known caves open to view, in six unknown caves, in six secret caves, and in two others," his biography tells us.

In addition to *The Tibetan Book of the Dead*, many of Guru Rinpoche's teachings were buried in caves, and he meditated in caves throughout Tibet, India, Nepal, and Bhutan. In these caves, it is believed, you can see signs and symbols—including Guru Rinpoche's handprints and footprints—and discover their attendant wisdom if you have the right perspective.

According to family lore, one of our ancestors meditated in a cave by the ancient pilgrimage site of Lake Manasarovar in Tibet and saw Guru Rinpoche's handprint on the surface of the blue waters, along with *Om* in Tibetan script, the sacred syllable that opens us to the nature of reality and uncharted spheres of consciousness. We're familiar with the idea of exploring outer space and finding planets and galaxies; in the bardo of a cave, we can make discoveries as we travel our inner universe.

~

The cave as a fertile bardo experience resonates with *ma*, a fundamental concept in Japanese culture. Ma means "interval" or "opening," both in space and time. Often referred to as negative (empty) space, it's positive in that it can birth something new. An invitation to heightened awareness, it's seen, for instance, as open space in rooms and gardens. With regard to time, it's a pause that invites contemplation. Ma is found in unpainted areas on folding screens, void areas in a photograph, silence during conversation, the hush between breaking waves. It's about the vitality generated by emptiness, in the way a blank page gives rise to creative energy. It's about being in relationship, because our engagement with ma allows fresh perspectives to emerge.

"In traditional Japanese space," says architect Kengo Kuma, "the most important space is the void. We call that kind of void space *ma*. In the void, we can feel the change of light, the change of time, the change of smell, the change of temperature.... The void and the human body are working together to feel something." The character for ma is "gate" (門) together with "sun" (日): 間. It evokes light filtering through a doorway, an idea suggested by Jun'ichirō Tanizaki in his essay about the Japanese aesthetic tradition, *In Praise of Shadows*, which I fell in love with when I lived in the teahouse. "The light from the garden steals in but dimly through paper-paneled doors," Tanizaki writes, "and it is precisely this indirect light that makes for us the charm of a room."

Like a simple Buddhist cave, my Tokyo teahouse was ma: no furniture, only the fragrant smell of the straw *tatami* mat floor, the light from the garden filtering through the *shōji* paper-paneled sliding doors. The teahouse was also ma because I lived there in the 1980s, before the Internet and smartphones and social media, and I didn't own a TV or a radio. It was a space in which I discovered fresh outlooks on nature, my girlhood, and feeling at home in the world.

During the COVID-19 pandemic, I had a ma experience in Kyoto that will likely never occur again. It was November, a time when the city is usually heaving with tourists come to admire the fall foliage, but Japan was closed to foreign visitors. Eager to explore this unprecedented bardo interval in the Japanese city I love most, I boarded the bullet train at Tokyo Station and a few hours later was in Kyoto.

I went to Ryōan-ji Temple to see the *mutei*, or garden of emptiness. Though it draws over a million people every year, I was alone on the wooden veranda, contemplating the fifteen big rocks surrounded by white gravel raked into flowing patterns. I'd been to the garden many times, but in the silence I was aware of what Kuma describes as the void and the body working together to feel something. I felt the light sifting through the surrounding trees, the changing shadows on the gravel that swirled around the rocks. I felt the air grow cold as the sun sank.

Crossing to the eastern side of the city, I walked up a winding stone-paved lane to Kiyomizu-dera Temple. The street was deserted, the shops selling souvenirs, antiques, and traditional sweets shuttered. When I reached the temple, a guard called out effusive greetings, perhaps grateful for company on this strangely still afternoon. Candles glowed in the main hall, with its statue of the thousand-armed Bodhisattva Kannon, and the smell of burning leaves drifted from the surrounding wooded area.

Outside on the temple platform, I watched twilight fall over the ancient city, Heian-kyō, the imperial capital of Japan for over a thousand years. On nights like this centuries before, the nobles of the Heian court exchanged lines of poetry imbued with *mono no aware*, a sensitivity to things, a sensibility of the sadness of things, an apprehension of evanescent beauty. *Mono no aware* was heightened in autumn, when things were dying, winding down and away, the world spinning ever more slowly in the approach to winter. "Even in Kyoto, / how I long for old Kyoto / when the cuckoo sings," Bashō wrote in a haiku famous for its bittersweet evocation of what's here and what's gone, of what perhaps never was or will be. I always sensed the intertwining of beauty and sadness when I visited Kyoto, but now, in the space of the quiet evening, I felt it especially keenly.

Ma makes me think of something my father showed me once when I was visiting him at his apartment in San Francisco. He turned off the lights and put a sake flask on the table. If I gazed directly at the flask, I couldn't see it, but if I looked to one side, the flask materialized. My father gave a detailed explanation about rod cells in the retina that, when the light is dim, allow you to perceive objects by focusing on the empty space next to them. What's stayed with me, though, is how in void space, the invisible can become visible, just as in the space of ma, in the cave, what we usually don't see can come into view.

~

Like the rinpoche from Ghoom who went to a cave near Tibet, we can "get power" by retreating to a bardo between-state. I dream sometimes that I'm discovering unused rooms in my house: *Here's a big empty room! How could I not have known about it? Why haven't I expanded into it? And here's another, and another!* The rooms are always back rooms that I reach by going down hallways I haven't noticed before.

One of my favorite essays by Montaigne, "On Solitude," describes a private space, an *arrière boutique* or back room, where we can ruminate: "We should set aside a room, just for ourselves, at the back of the shop, keeping it entirely free and establishing there our true liberty, our principal solitude and asylum." Montaigne discusses the arrière boutique in relation to impermanence, as a place where we can become accustomed to being alone, away from partner and children and friends, "so that when the occasion arises that we must lose them it should not be a new experience to do without them." At the same time, it was a place where he could muse and ponder and write, giving free rein to his imagination.

Montaigne's arrière boutique was the library in his château that he retreated to after retiring in 1570 from the Bordeaux *parlement*, the tower library that my father visited when he was a student in Paris in the 1950s. In this aerie, Montaigne kept items he had inherited from his ancestors—an escritoire, a prayer book, a sword—and curios from distant shores.

I like to think that my study, where I go to reflect and write, is similar to Montaigne's. There's a Tibetan *gau* charm box that my ancestors carried on journeys for protection; my grandfather's prayer book, with a note inside from my grandmother ("To my dear old hubby with my best love and kisses from your beloved wife, 3rd July 1939"); the mandala-patterned saddle rug my great-grandfather used when he rode across the Tibetan Plateau; my father's copy of Montaigne's *Essais*, the binding taped and retaped, with my father's personal stamp on the flyleaf. I'm also surrounded by objects from my travels: carved Balinese dolls, a sandalwood elephant from Rajasthan, a Mexican Day of the Dead tableau of tuxedoed skeletons playing guitars and trumpets.

The arrière boutique is a space all to yourself, a ma void space where you can go to the cave and explore. Where might yours be? Perhaps it's a study, a reading nook, a screened-off area in your house, a shed in the garden (when I was small, my back room was under the arching branches of a giant forsythia bush in our yard). The arrière boutique can also be experienced by doing things that generate a feeling of flow, a sense of opening space in your mind. This can be through journaling or reading poetry; knitting, gardening, or woodworking. As a girl, I loved to sew. With the passing hours, I discovered new thoughts and ideas, sinking deeper and deeper into myself as I pinned the tissue paper pattern to the fabric, cut and stitched, often until dawn.

Transformational as going to the cave can be, we may not love it—at least initially. On retreat in a cave, Milarepa, weak from hunger, went out to collect wood so he could make a cooking fire. When he returned, he found that a host of wrathful beings had taken up residence, "iron-*atsaras* [demons] sitting with eyes agape, the size of saucers." In *Magic and Mystery in Tibet*, Alexandra David-Néel describes how, from November 1914 to August 1916, she sought enlightenment by retreating to a "small-sized cave closed by a wall of uncemented stones, in which two narrow gaping holes less than ten inches high served for windows," twelve thousand feet above sea level in Sikkim. Her cave was snowed in throughout the long, punishing winter; once a day, a meal was left at the entrance by someone she never saw. She writes, "My life resembled that of the Carthusians without the diversion which they may find in attendance at religious services."

When he retired, Montaigne looked forward to his life of contemplation, but as M. A. Screech explains in the introduction to his translation of *Essais*, "Montaigne's project of calm study soon went wrong. He fell into an unbalanced melancholy; his spirit galloped off like a runaway horse; his mind, left fallow, produced weeds not grass." In the 1950s, with the proceeds from the film rights to her novel *The Sea Wall*, Marguerite Duras bought an old stone house in Neauphle-le-Château, a village about an hour southwest of Paris. There were lace curtains, dried flowers in jars, black-and-white tile floors, a tall mirror reflecting doorways through doorways, like a reflection of the mind. "I was alone in this house," Duras recounts in *Writing*. "I shut myself in—of course, I was afraid."

When we decide to enter the cave, wherever and whatever it may be, we often struggle at first. Why are we there instead of doing something—anything—easier and more enjoyable? If we persevere, though, new perspectives can arise. Milarepa tried to chase the iron-atsaras from his cave, but "some of them bared their fangs wrathfully. Several laughed and yelled with booming voice. Together, all of them swiped and stabbed in the air, attempting to intimidate Milarepa." Then he sang,

> You band of ghosts, demons, and obstructing spirits here,
> How sublime it is that you've come at this time.
> Don't hurry; relax and stay for a while.
> Let's chat about everything under the sun.
> You're hurried? Aw! You can stay just one night!

The demons vanished, and Milarepa understood that they were projections from his mind, that the way to free himself from inner obstructions like greed, anger, and delusion was through surrender rather than resistance.

By the time spring arrived in the Himalayas, the "tenacious snows" melting and wildflowers blooming, David-Néel had come to revel in her seclusion. "Solitude, solitude!" she exulted. "Mind and senses develop their sensibility in this contemplative life made up of continual observations and reflections. Does one become a visionary or, rather, is it not that one has been blind until then?"

For Montaigne, Screech tells us, "writing the *Essays* was...a successful attempt to exorcize [his melancholy]." Recording his thoughts and feelings (a practice that was groundbreaking in the sixteenth century, when there existed a "taboo against writing primarily about oneself"), Montaigne not only came to know himself better and moved toward "a full and joyful acceptance of life" but also produced a seminal masterpiece.

As for Duras, she stayed on in the Neauphle-le-Château house, alone at her desk. "And then," she writes in a passage that echoes the concept of ma and Tanizaki's *In Praise of Shadows*, "I began to love it. This house became the house of writing. My books come from this house. From this light as well, and from the garden. From the light reflecting off the pond."

If Milarepa, David-Néel, Montaigne, and Duras had abandoned their chosen caves rather than persisting, they wouldn't have undergone the profound shifts in understanding that allowed them to live with greater authenticity and contentment. In day-to-day life, we can take this bardo lesson to heart by making space for free-form reflection, entering our arrière boutique—a room in your house, space in your mind as you make breakfast or commute to work, a cabin in the woods—and persevering through whatever challenges arise. When I feel like this is too difficult, I think about the Darjeeling monks who went to the cave and what their experience must have been like. Contending with hunger and fatigue, heat and cold, insects and snakes and wild animals, they stayed until spring, open to new ways of seeing.

~

We can also experience transformation if we're thrust into the cave against our will instead of entering it intentionally. When my great-grandfather was buried in the snow, with only minutes remaining before he suffocated, he located courage in the teachings of Guru Rinpoche. Ill with endocarditis, I despaired of finding a way out of my terrible predicament, but discovered hope in the story I'd forgotten about my great-grandfather and the avalanche.

When my father's death in the fall of 2012 plunged me into bardo, it didn't seem possible that any light could shine into that dark space. I'd look through the things that I'd brought back to Tokyo after he died—his striped shirt, the *Paris des rêves* book of photographs and poems, his birding binoculars—but this only intensified my suffering.

At some point, though, I found myself reflecting with gratitude rather than grief on what we'd shared. It might have been around the time of the Japanese *Obon* festival the following August, as people in the neighborhood lit *chōchin* lanterns to guide the spirits of their ancestors back home for a few days of celebration and commemoration. I felt a release, the sense that I could start letting go of my father as my parent and welcoming him as my ancestor. Japanese friends had told me when my father died that it takes about a year to mourn, and this was indeed what I experienced.

Beautiful memories started coming back to me, especially of our road trips across America when I was a girl. My father loved driving at night, and I'd ride shotgun while the rest of the family slept; it was just the two of us talking as the hours and miles flowed past, my father's face lit by the glow of the dashboard. I learned from my father about conversation as exploratory, in the spirit of Montaigne's "De l'art de conférer" ("On the Art of Conversation"), surely one of the *Essais* my father liked best. "To my taste the most fruitful and most natural exercise of our minds is conversation," Montaigne writes. "I find the practice of it the most delightful activity in our lives." Now, as I went about my everyday Tokyo existence of family and writing and teaching, I felt my conversation with my father continuing as I examined and considered, in dialogue with him, myself, and others. To my surprise and delight, I discovered that even though my father was gone, I hadn't lost him.

In my interviews with writers about bardo, I've heard moving stories about the alchemy that can take place when we're pitched into the between, narratives that have deepened the insights I've gained from my own experiences with being thrust into the cave.

"I woke up one morning in 2021 and couldn't see out of my right eye," Julia Alvarez told me. "It was like palm branches tumbling down inside the eye and then it went all black." Alvarez had suffered a retinal detachment, which is a rare, often sudden emergency condition. "I had to undergo two major surgeries, each of them five hours of excruciating pain," she said. "Afterward, I was put in a contraption for eight days, face down, with a little slot to feed myself. At night in bed, there was a brace for me to put my head in."

The surgeries failed, and Alvarez was forced to accept that she'd lost sight in her eye. "For a while, all I could talk about was what had happened to me," she said. "And then someone told me about something challenging that they were dealing with and I thought, 'Oh, we're all going through our own struggles.' I suddenly felt compassion, such compassion. It's a privileged position to think, 'Why me?' Because it's, 'Why all of us?'"

Alvarez has also arrived at fresh wisdom as an author. Her latest novel, *The Cemetery of Untold Stories*, is about an aging Dominican American writer who returns to the Dominican Republic after many years in the United States to bury the manuscripts she hasn't been able to finish. It was through the bardo of losing sight in her eye that

Alvarez discovered how to complete the book, which had come to an impasse, as she understood that her own time as a writer will end and she won't be able to tell all the stories she wants to tell. "How do you come to terms with that?" she said. "The way I have is that I don't feel it's, 'Après moi, le silence.' It's, 'Après moi, other storytellers.' It's not that I, with my name on it, have to get the stories told. The stories, the storytellers will continue."

Author David James Duncan found greater understanding when his beloved seventeen-year-old brother, John, died following open-heart surgery. In his classic essay, "The Mickey Mantle Koan," Duncan writes about how, when John was dying, their mother asked John's hero, Mickey Mantle, to send him an autographed baseball. It arrived the day of John's embalmment, inscribed:

<blockquote>
To John—
My Best Wishes
Your Pal
Mickey Mantle

April 6, 1965
</blockquote>

Devastated by the loss of his brother, Duncan expected the baseball to have a healing effect, but that didn't happen. Instead it came to seem like a Zen Buddhist koan, a riddle that can lead to enlightenment. He sensed that the transformation he longed for wouldn't be conferred by the ball itself but by the distance between "one of the beat-up, earth-colored, grass-scented balls that had given [me and John] such happiness, and this antiseptic-smelling, sad-making, icon-ball."

Then, Duncan told me, he had an epiphany:

> Looking out the window at where John and I used to play, ... I saw my brother catch, then throw, a baseball. It was that simple. In that moment, I remembered how little John and I had needed to be happy: two scuffed-up old mitts and a grass-stained ball. I then fell through a floor inside myself, landing in a deeper, brighter chamber in which something much more than brotherly love was conveyed: *Who's to say we need even an old ball to be happy? Who's to say we can't do with less? Who's to say we can't* still *be happy—with no ball at all? And I was happy.* ... And with that wave of happiness, the koan was solved.

In his essay, Duncan writes, "I find it more than a little consoling to recall my encounter, one October day, with an unspeakable spark in me that needs *nothing*—not even a dog-eared ball—to be happy."

When his life changed abruptly after 9/11 as people viewed him with suspicion, writer Mohsin Hamid at first resisted his startling, unwelcome reality, but then he discovered another way of seeing. "After a while, I began to ask myself if the normal I wanted to return to was such a desirable situation," Hamid told me. "Should I instead scrutinize more closely how things are and the degree to which I myself have been complicit? This gave birth to *The Reluctant Fundamentalist*, my novel about a character who works in New York City around 9/11, went to Princeton, and feels he has to make a choice. Should he be Pakistani, should he be American, should he connect with Islamic sensibilities?"

The insight Hamid gained from his experience also informs his latest novel, *The Last White Man*. When the protagonist, Anders, finds one morning that he has turned brown, he's thrown into a harrowing liminal state. "It's a story of the ending of something," Hamid said. "But it also suggests that every ending is a beginning, and by focusing with so much fear on the endings that we face, we're perhaps missing an openness to the idea that there could be some beginnings, and they might be worth exploring."

These days, I'm in an involuntary bardo as I witness my mother's decline. Not long ago, she fell and broke her femur, and I flew from Tokyo to San Francisco to help take care of her. Every day from 7 a.m. to 3 p.m., I sat at her bedside in the skilled nursing facility where she was recovering after surgery. I'd leave the house at 6:30 and drive north on Highway 101, the moon setting in the indigo sky over Mount Tam.

I sat with my mother, holding her hand, and we dozed and talked and watched TV. I thought about how over fifty years earlier, she had held me at the naval hospital in Andalusia when I was born, the two of us sleeping as the moon set over the Strait of Gibraltar and the *levante* wind blew in from Africa.

My mother's mind roamed, set loose by her cognitive decline and the pain medication she was being given at the nursing facility.

"Do you want to go somewhere in the air with me?" she asked one day, looking up at the sunlit clouds as I pushed her around the courtyard in her wheelchair. "I wish I could fly."

Gazing out the window from her bed on a cold, gray morning, she said, "Times have changed. I've become terribly old."

She couldn't find one of her hearing aids. "There's nothing that replaces what you've lost."

She used to make prizeworthy baked goods, like the cruise ship cake she created for my fifth birthday, complete with Life Savers for portholes. Now, she wondered where her Julia Child cookbook was, because she wanted to whip up a chocolate mousse.

We got to talking about her childhood in Darjeeling and I asked if she was missing India. "No, because I have pictures of Mount Kanchenjunga in my room. That's all I need. I love America." She needed, though, to write a letter to her parents: "I saw them off, but I want to make sure they arrived safely."

We talked about how she journeyed to America, became a doctor, and raised four children. She said, "I've had a life of wonderment."

One night, I dream that my mother and I are at a train station. She stands by the tracks wearing dark sunglasses and a sun hat. She's waving goodbye to me, her expression resolute, because we can't stay together in this life forever. Her expression is matter-of-fact, like: *Be well.*

When we went back to India on that final trip and she arranged the prayer ceremony for her mother, I asked what rituals she'd like done when she's gone. "Do you want us to scatter your ashes in the Teesta River?"

"I'd like you to throw them in the Pacific." We could hire a boat, she said, to take us out past the Golden Gate Bridge to where the ocean flows freely. Afterward, we must invite people over for a reception with nibbles and drinks. At the thought of a gathering like that, the kind my mother would be beautifully in charge of—where, when everyone had left, we'd chat in the kitchen over the last bit of coffee in the Chemex—I felt overwhelming sorrow.

Little by little, though, my perspective is shifting, and the light of gratitude and acceptance is filtering in.

~

We not only face adversity and find insight individually but also collectively. Amid the communal suffering unleashed by Japan's 3/11 earthquake and tsunami, photographer Munemasa Takahashi started the Lost & Found Project, a traveling exhibition of photos that had been recovered after the disaster but were too damaged to identify and return to their owners. The photos had been put in the "Hopeless Box," but Takahashi felt they had the power to speak about the catastrophe in human terms, beyond the numbers (the size of the quake, the height of the tsunami, how many were dead or missing) that were being cited by the media in sensational reports soon to be supplanted by the next big story. In his book about the project, *Tsunami, Photographs, and Then*, Takahashi explains, "Nobody was trying to deliver the death right in front of people's eyes. Nobody said to people, 'You may die soon too.'"

The Lost & Found photos were exhibited around the world, in Australia, the United States, Spain, Italy. People wept as they gazed at the spectral, swirling images of families and friends, of ordinary lives cut short. The photos were reminders of both presence and absence, our desire to remember and be remembered even as we know—or perhaps because we know—that eventually everything we love will vanish.

By putting an intimate, personal face on a tragedy of such monumental proportions, the exhibits made possible a shared mourning. They allowed people to grieve for all who suffered from 3/11, as well as to reflect on their own losses; to discover new ways of interacting with communal grief and our status as travelers in a world of impermanence. "What this project told us," Takahashi writes, "was that when something happens which is totally out of our hands, instead of being overcome with a feeling of helplessness, individuals taking small steps will collectively bring positive results."

When the COVID-19 pandemic hit, we were all catapulted out of our usual lives into a global bardo. Schools shut down and classes went online, restaurants closed, people lost their jobs or started working remotely, plans for holidays and celebrations were canceled. As we grappled with illness and isolation, grief and longing to return to the existence we'd known, we also had the chance to alchemize our suffering into greater compassion for others and understanding of interconnectedness in our communities and on our planet.

At the beginning of the pandemic in early 2020, Henry was in his sophomore year at university in the United

States. He returned home to Tokyo and took classes on Zoom in the middle of the night with his faithful study buddy, Mac, next to him. I felt deeply unhappy that his college experience was being interrupted, and, at the same time, I worried about my mother sequestered at her retirement home in California, my daughter sheltering in place in New York, the worldwide death toll, and growing anti-Asian sentiment.

Every night over dinner, Henry talked with me and David about the economic inequality exacerbated by the pandemic; George Floyd and Black Lives Matter and the movement to defund the police; the work he was doing on campus with census outreach and voter registration; his excitement about the Biden administration. Those conversations showed me what it means to locate hope during difficult times. For my son and his peers, life had been put on pause, but their minds and hearts had not. Our pandemic dinner conversations sometimes erupted into arguments as Henry challenged and pushed us. I worried about this, too—I didn't want to cause him any more stress than he was already feeling—but he helped me see our disagreements differently. One night when the discussion grew especially heated, I told him I didn't want our relationship to be adversarial. "We're not against each other!" he said, surprised. "We're side by side."

Whether we're thrown into an unwanted bardo individually or collectively, we can work to accept what has happened and be open to new interpretations and insight. This doesn't mean we won't feel grief and pain, but that what we learn in the cave can lead to a more authentic engagement with ourselves and the world when, like Tibetan *déloks*, we return from the beyond. Our fresh perspective can guide us through the next bardo within life that we'll no doubt experience, as well as on our day-to-day journey through the bardo from birth to death.

At caves in Tibet where Guru Rinpoche is said to have meditated, pilgrims who want to hold close the wisdom associated with the sites they've visited might take home a bit of soil, a leaf, or a sacred object. When I traveled to Lhasa in the 1980s, I was given a *tsatsa* clay sculpture at Palhalupuk, a cave temple said to have been a meditation retreat for the seventh-century king Songtsen Gampo, who laid the foundation for Buddhism in Tibet and is revered as an incarnation of Chenrezig, Bodhisattva of Compassion. The cave is near the site of the old Western Gate, which my grandmother rode through on her pony when she entered the holy city, bells strung from the top of the gate tinkling in the May wind.

Now, over sixty years later, I was exchanging greetings with two young monks at Palhalupuk, just as my grandmother would have. The monks presented me with a small tsatsa of Yama, Lord of Death, who is an aspect of

Chenrezig. It sits on a shelf in my study today as I write these words, here to remind me that everything changes and ends, and that impermanence need not be feared. We feel we must gird ourselves against impermanence in order to be happy but, as I learned when I was ill, true joy is found by embracing it.

Keeping objects that remind us of what we've learned in bardo is a powerful way to chart our course. They might include a baseball or a copy of Tanizaki's *In Praise of Shadows*, a rock found on a visit to your ancestors' hometown, a photograph taken from your window during the pandemic. Serving as a kind of personal lexicon, objects like these help us put the knowledge we've gained into practice and find greater contentment day to day.

⁓

Bardos within life, and the bardo from birth to death, are like ma, like the cave in southern India where the Darjeeling monks went on retreat, like the cave where *The Tibetan Book of the Dead* was hidden. Charged with possibility, they're liminal spaces where we can perceive the reality of things. They're spaces with boundaries, not like a closed box, but like a Japanese teahouse, which has walls and a roof yet is open to air and light.

Our journey through bardo is potentially a great work of art and we are the artists, creating our path forward. The fundamental reason, I think, for the enduring popularity of *The Tibetan Book of the Dead* is that it shows us how we can be the artists of our lives and find the happiness we long for. This longing can be seen as a kind of age-old yearning for paradise, for a place of refuge in a world of uncertainty and change.

Tibetan Buddhist texts speak to this desire, telling of secret paradise valleys known as *beyul*. Blessed by Guru Rinpoche and located on both geographical and spiritual planes, they're utopian realms that can be reached through portals on mountaintops and behind waterfalls, in dreams and the mind. Countless obstacles are said to arise as we search for them. Many seekers lose their way in harsh terrain; they're attacked by bandits or predatory beasts, forced back by extreme weather. Internal obstacles such as attachment, delusion, and distraction can keep us from seeing a beyul even if we're standing right in front of it, just as Guru Rinpoche's handprints and footprints are only visible if you have the right view.

One beyul that Buddhist pilgrims have long searched for is Shambhala, a kingdom of peace and harmony written about in a text called the *Kalachakra Tantra*. Shambhala likely served as the inspiration for James Hilton's best-selling novel *Lost Horizon* (1933), the story of a British consul who crash-lands in Tibet and finds sanctuary at a lamasery called Shangri-La, where one can "achieve calmness and profundity, ripeness and wisdom." Chögyam

Trungpa, a Tibetan rinpoche renowned for teaching about Shambhala, said the kingdom can be seen "not as an external place, but as the ground or root of wakefulness and sanity that exists as a potential within every human being."

However much we may wish to realize this potential, the prospect of leaving our comfort zones of body, mind, and speech can be daunting. In bardo, *The Tibetan Book of the Dead* says, we're tempted away from the wisdom available to us toward the realms of samsaric suffering: "A dull, smoke-coloured light from Hell will shine alongside the light of the Mirror-like Wisdom and will also strike against thee. Thereupon,... thou wilt beget fear and be startled at the dazzling white light and wilt wish to flee from it; thou wilt beget a feeling of fondness for the dull smoke-coloured light from Hell."

Similarly, when we encounter the awakened mind in the form of the Clear Light of Reality, we may fail to embrace it. In a footnote, Evans-Wentz explains, "The consciousness-principle of the average human being lacks the power to function in [a condition of balance]; *karmic* propensities becloud the consciousness-principle... and, losing equilibrium, the consciousness-principle falls away from the Clear Light.... [A]nd so the Wheel of Life continues to turn."

The Wheel turns and turns, but at any moment we can release ourselves from the cycle. The words of *The Tibetan Book of the Dead* may at first seem harsh: "Abandon egotism," we're told, "abandon propensities... be not weak."

And: "Such misery thou wilt be experiencing at present. But feeling miserable will avail thee nothing now."

One of the most moving and powerful aspects of the teaching, though, is that it's also meant to comfort us. Eighth-century tough love powered by compassion, it has guided and consoled both the dead and the living for hundreds of years. Listening to the steady rise and fall of the lamas' deep, measured voices as they read the ancient words of wisdom, we're reassured: *Here we are together in this fleeting world.* The lamas remain by our side, companions—like the teaching—along the way.

*The Tibetan Book of the Dead* counsels, "The training... being of particular importance even while living, hold to it, read it, commit it to memory, bear it in mind properly, read it regularly thrice; let the words and the meanings be very clear; it should be so that the words and the meanings will not be forgotten even though a hundred executioners were pursuing thee."

In closing, the book says,

> One should not forget [the teaching's] meaning and the words, even though pursued by seven mastiffs.
>
> By this Select Teaching, one obtaineth Buddhahood at the moment of death. Were the Buddhas of the Three Times [the Past, the Present, and the Future] to seek, [they] could not find any doctrine transcending this.

Thus is completed the Profound Heart-Drops of the *Bardo* Doctrine, called *The Bardo Thödol*, which liberateth embodied beings.

The ancient Tibetan scriptures say that paradise is there if only we will see it. Liberation is there for us if only we will work *for* rather than against it in our lives. The potential for lasting happiness lies in breaking free into our full humanity. When Prince Gautama left the cloistered palace to go out into the world, he was driven by the urge to understand the dimensions of human existence. He knew his father wanted him to one day be king, and he knew he couldn't live that life.

As Gautama realized when he attained enlightenment and became the Buddha, freedom means relinquishing what's no longer right for us (or never was). It means practicing renunciation in the best of ways, giving up habitual actions that have made happiness elusive, and opening ourselves to reality. It means embracing our precious human life, not because we're afraid we will lose it, but because we are fortunate enough to have it at all. The challenge and hope for us as we travel in bardo is that we confirm our humanity by living the life that's ours to live.

# EPILOGUE

After finishing the translation of the *Bardo Thödol*, Lama Kazi Dawa-Samdup took a position as a lecturer in Tibetan at the University of Calcutta, but he would not live to see *The Tibetan Book of the Dead* in print. "Very unfortunately, as is usual with peoples habituated to the high Himalayan regions," W. Y. Evans-Wentz noted in his introduction, "he lost his health completely in the tropical climate of Calcutta, and departed from this world on the twenty-second day of March, 1922."

Evans-Wentz would go on to write and publish books related to Tibetan Buddhism as he traveled between India, England, and America. In 1941, as World War II accelerated, he journeyed by ship from India to New York and then crossed the country to San Diego, where he'd lived as a young man, and took a room downtown at the Keystone Hotel. He thought about returning to the Himalayas, but never did. He led a quiet life: eating vegetarian food, reading at the public library, and spending

## EPILOGUE

time at Cuchama, a mountain on the border with Mexico that he felt had exceptional spiritual power. When he died in 1965, *The Tibetan Book of the Dead* was read at his funeral, and his ashes were interred in a stupa in India looking out toward the mountains.

I wonder how often Evans-Wentz thought about that rainy day in 1919 when he walked to Gangtok with my great-grandfather's letter of introduction in his bag. On long afternoons at the San Diego library, meditating beneath the moon at Cuchama, did he marvel at how unexpectedly he and Lama Kazi Dawa-Samdup had helped bring Buddhism to the West, at how the old manuscripts they'd studied and discussed on chilly mornings over endless cups of tea had changed the lives of generations?

As for S. W. Laden La, he would dedicate his life to diplomatic, philanthropic, and religious endeavors. In 1920, he made his first visit to Lhasa, as secretary to a mission led by Sir Charles Bell, who had served as the Political Officer for Sikkim, Bhutan, and Tibet. My great-grandfather had developed a deep personal devotion to the Dalai Lama when His Holiness took refuge in Darjeeling in 1910, and on the visit to Lhasa with Bell, his biography reports, "it was an awe-inspiring experience for him to have an audience with the Dalai Lama in the [Potala Palace]. He regarded it as an enormous privilege and responsibility, and every detail of his visit to the Potala was recorded in his personal diary with great reverence." When he returned to Tibet in

# EPILOGUE

1923 to establish a police force as part of the Dalai Lama's effort to modernize the country, Laden La wrote to his son:

> You will be glad to hear that His Holiness the Dalai Lama has appointed me as the Chief-of-Police in Tibet. In appointing me as such he has conferred on me the title of Dzasa—which is equal to Lord or Peer in English.
>
> I received the order about my high appointment on the 2.11.23—and according to Tibetan custom His Holiness, who is the King of Tibet—received me in audience on the 11th and conferred on me the title according to ancient custom by putting round my neck a large silk scarf. After conferment of the title he received me privately in his beautiful garden house which stands in the middle of a lake where I had a long conversation for about one and a half hours.

In 1930, Laden La visited Lhasa twice more to carry out diplomatic work. At the end of his final stay, on September 20, 1930, he bid farewell to the Dalai Lama. He later recorded in his diary that they spent the afternoon together "and had interesting talks.... He was very kind to me and blessed me with a large scarf and blue blessed silk knots." After praying one last time at the Jokhang Temple, my great-grandfather mounted his pony and set off for home.

## EPILOGUE

He broke the weeks-long journey to India at remote dak bungalows, riding out every morning at dawn and stopping before the terrible winds rose that could blow a man right off his horse. He ate a simple dinner, noted the day's events in his diary by lamplight, prayed to Guru Rinpoche, and then drifted to sleep under the star-scattered sky.

Back in Darjeeling, Laden La soon retired and turned his attention to local politics, charitable work, social activities (such as racing his horses at Lebong, "the smallest, highest and crookedest racecourse in the world"), and Buddhism. He maintained a regular correspondence with the Dalai Lama until His Holiness's death in 1933, exchanging perspectives on regional and global affairs. Eager to represent the interests of the Darjeeling hill people in their quest for greater autonomy, he ran for the local assembly, but this was not to be. His biography recounts, "On Christmas Day 1936, he made the journey to canvass for votes in Kalimpong.... In Kalimpong, he received a very warm reception from his supporters, and he made a fine speech, but it must have been all too much for his health. That night, without any warning, he died in his sleep at the age of sixty."

In the introduction to Laden La's translation of Guru Rinpoche's biography, Evans-Wentz writes, "Nothing is known either of the origin or of the end of [Guru Rinpoche].

# EPILOGUE

According to tradition, [he is] believed never to have died." In a similar way, the wisdom of *The Tibetan Book of the Dead* lives on, just as Guru Rinpoche intended and my great-grandfather fervently hoped.

I carry forward my great-grandfather's work in whatever ways I can. On my desk, I keep a reminder of his legacy: his prayer beads, which were given to my grandmother after he died and then to me after her death, the same ones he thrust through the snow that winter morning in Tibet. I think often of my grandmother praying with these beads in her little wooden house, the peaks of Kanchenjunga brilliant white against the turquoise sky, and beyond, the great Tibetan Plateau. I hear her low, rhythmic chanting, and smell the burning butter lamps and incense. I see the sun illuminating the old altar painted with the Tibetan lucky symbols, the statues of Guru Rinpoche and the past and future Buddhas golden in the reflected light.

# ACKNOWLEDGMENTS

Deepest thanks to all who have supported me on the bardo journey to the publication of this book. Ellen Scordato, my brilliant agent, who gave me The Idea over lunch that summer day in Manhattan. Lisa Weinert, for showing me a way forward with her next-level thinking. The incredible team at Hachette: Renée Sedliar, Nzinga Temu, Carrie Napolitano, Gwen Hawkes, Sean Moreau, Alexandra Hernandez, Maya Lewis, Alana Spendley, and Hayley Silverman. Heeyah Design for the gorgeous cover. Kathy Streckfus for her wonderful copyediting. Kay Mariea and Erica Lawrence for their meticulous proofreading. The incomparable Aileen Boyle and Brian Ulicky, for helping bring this book into the world.

Thank you to James Shaheen for his support of my work and for saying yes to a bardo interview series at *Tricycle*. To all the interviewees for so generously sharing their perspectives on bardo and the art of living. Heartfelt thanks to Dani Shapiro for her kindness, support, and friendship. Thank you to Kim Adrian, Martin Alexander, Julia Alvarez, Jon Lee Anderson, Michelle

## ACKNOWLEDGMENTS

Anderson, Frederick Barthelme, Charles Baxter, Andrea Beauchamp, Ruth Behar, Lisa Belkin, Sven Birkerts, Bianca Bosker, Kimberly Burns, Nicole Chung, Sandra Cisneros, Nicholas Delbanco, Amanda Dennis, Junot Diaz, Tenzin Dickie, Mary Duncan, John Einarsen, Melissa Febos, Elizabeth Gilbert, Lauren Grodstein, Mohsin Hamid, Zach Helfand, Gail Hochman, Yuka Igarashi, Amy Joyce, Jody Kahn, Alice Kandell, Porochista Khakpour, Perri Klass, Mimi Kusch, Sanaë Lemoine, Megan Marshall, Elyse Michaels-Berger, Lorrie Moore, Maud Newton, Dan Piepenbring, Bill Pierce, Allison Markin Powell, Anne Redmon, Ken Rodgers, Phil Ryan, Sharon Salzberg, David Sedaris, Mike Sheffield, Rod Smith, Allison Slater Tate, Robert Thurman, Deborah Treisman, Michelle Wildgen, and Roberta Zeff.

Special thanks to Tashi Chodron at the Rubin Museum of Himalayan Art for inviting me to share my writing and my Tibetan family story. Thank you to Raghu Markus, host of the *Mindrolling* podcast (Be Here Now Network). Anita Gupta, host of the *Post-Call: Frontline Health Stories* podcast. Livia McCarthy, director of alumni engagement, and Margaret Miller, retired deputy vice president for alumni affairs, Princeton University. Lauran Hartley, director of the Modern Tibetan Studies Program, Weatherhead East Asian Institute, Columbia University. Clare Harris, professor of visual anthropology and curator for

# ACKNOWLEDGMENTS

Asian Collections at the Pitt Rivers Museum, University of Oxford. Gail Finley and Asia Society Texas Center. Jaina Sanga and The Dallas Institute of Humanities and Culture.

Gratitude to the lamas in Darjeeling who so patiently answered my many, many questions.

Thank you to Peter Johnson and John McPhee for their wise counsel and friendship over these many years. Alain Youell, for helping me find my way through bardo. Cynthia Davis, Sherab Tenduf, Paula Hines, Jim and Joyce Javid, Jonathan Slater, Ann Watson. Valerie Koehn, Brad Schwarz, Alasdair Bowie, Steve Hesse, Peter Nadler, Grace Sekimitsu. Kimiyo and Shiro Kondo. My colleagues at Japan Women's University for their kindness and support.

Thank you to my brave, brilliant, and beautiful mother, Tenki Tenduf La, for showing me how to pursue your dreams (and take time to rumba while you're at it). My father, John Davis, who taught me about the life of the mind and the back roads of Provence, about how to live according to a motto that his hero, Montaigne, lived by: *Summum nec metuas diem, nec optes* (Neither be afraid of your last day nor desire it). My beloved grandmother, Phurpa Lhamu Tenduf La, for sharing her stories, and for showing me how to love life and take my chances as they come. My great-grandfather, S. W. Laden La, for inspiring me with his compassion and fortitude, and for giving W. Y. Evans-Wentz a letter of introduction to Lama Kazi

## ACKNOWLEDGMENTS

Dawa-Samdup in 1919 so the *Bardo Thödol* could be translated into English.

Thank you to my faithful writing assistants, Mac Hunter and Beau Dawa, for keeping me company through long hours of writing and reminding me when it's time to go for a walk. Sophia and Henry, my angels, for the happiness they bring me and the gift of their beautiful hearts. David, my love and life companion, who never, ever doubted. Since that rainy March night in Tokyo forty years ago, we've been walking side by side, and I'm thankful every day that we found each other.

Finally, it's a joy and an honor to share the wisdom of *The Tibetan Book of the Dead* with you in this book. *Kyi kyi so so lha gyal lo!* Safe passage to us all as we journey through life, travelers together in bardo.

Ann Tashi Slater

March 2025

Tokyo, Japan

# SOURCES AND WORKS CONSULTED

Quotations from *The Tibetan Book of the Dead* are from the third edition of the W. Y. Evans-Wentz and Lama Kazi Dawa-Samdup translation (Oxford University Press, 1960). Brackets in the original have been omitted, except where necessary for clarity.

Parts of this book appear in my previously published work, noted within this section.

Chapter 7 is based on "Traveling in Bardo," an essay I published in *AGNI* on October 15, 2017 (https://agnionline.bu.edu/essay/traveling-in-bardo). The content has been revised and expanded.

Excerpt from *The Year of Magical Thinking* by Joan Didion, copyright © 2005 by Joan Didion. Used by permission of Alfred A. Knopf, an imprint of the Knopf Doubleday Publishing Group, a division of Penguin Random House LLC. All rights reserved.

Excerpt from *The Year of Magical Thinking* by Joan Didion, copyright © 2005 by Joan Didion, used by permission of Janklow & Nesbit Associates, which controls audio rights.

Excerpt from *Girlhood* by Melissa Febos (Bloomsbury, © 2021) used by kind permission of the author.

Excerpt from *Silence: In the Age of Noise* by Erling Kagge, translation by Becky L. Crook, translation copyright © 2017 by Becky L. Crook. Used by permission of Pantheon Books, an imprint of the Knopf Doubleday Publishing Group, a division of Penguin Random House LLC. All rights reserved.

## SOURCES AND WORKS CONSULTED

Excerpt from *I Am Homeless if This Is Not My Home: A Novel* by Lorrie Moore, copyright © 2023 by Lorrie Moore. Used by permission of Alfred A. Knopf, an imprint of the Knopf Doubleday Publishing Group, a division of Penguin Random House LLC. All rights reserved.

Excerpt from *I Am Homeless if This Is Not My Home: A Novel* by Lorrie Moore, copyright © 2023 by Lorrie Moore. Used by permission of Listening Library, an imprint of Penguin Random House LLC. All rights reserved.

---

Alvarez, Julia. *The Cemetery of Untold Stories*. Algonquin Books, 2024.

———. "The Painful Beauty of Being Alive." Interview by author. "Between-States: Conversations About Bardo and Life." *Tricycle: The Buddhist Review*, September 26, 2024, https://tricycle.org/article/julia-alvarez.

Anderson, Laurie. "Laurie Anderson on Songs from the Bardo." Interview by Huib Schippers, April 3, 2018. Liner notes for Laurie Anderson, Tenzin Choegyal, and Jesse Paris Smith, *Songs from the Bardo*, 2019, available at Smithsonian Folkways Recordings, https://folkways-media.si.edu/docs/folkways/artwork/SFW40583.pdf.

Appiah, Kwame Anthony. "Princeton University Class of 2023 Baccalaureate Remarks by Kwame Anthony Appiah." Transcript of speech delivered at Princeton University, May 28, 2023, www.princeton.edu/news/2023/05/28/princeton-university-class-2023-baccalaureate-remarks-kwame-anthony-appiah.

Armstrong, Karen. *Buddha*. Orion Books, 2002.

Bakewell, Sarah. *How to Live: A Life of Montaigne in One Question and Twenty Attempts at an Answer*. Other Press, 2010.

Baldwin, James. "Go the Way Your Blood Beats." Interview by Richard Goldstein. In *James Baldwin: The Last Interview: and Other Conversations*. Melville House, 2014, Kindle edition.

## SOURCES AND WORKS CONSULTED

Bashō, Matsuo. *Narrow Road to the Interior and Other Writings.* Translated by Sam Hamill. Shambhala, 2000.

Bemelmans, Ludwig. *Madeline.* Puffin Books, 2000.

Child, Julia. *My Life in France.* Anchor Books, 2006.

Chögyam Trungpa. *Shambhala: The Sacred Path of the Warrior.* Shambhala, 2007.

Chōmei, Kamo no. *Hōjōki: A Hermit's Hut as Metaphor.* Translated by Matthew Stavros. 3rd ed. (for Kindle). Vicus Lusorum, 2020. Revised January 2023.

Dalai Lama, Tenzin Gyatso, [XIV]. *Advice on Dying: And Living a Better Life.* Translated by Jeffrey Hopkins. Atria Books, 2002.

———. (@DalaiLama). "Karma means action and action motivated by compassion is good. To complain that what happens to you is just the result of your karma is lazy. Instead, confidently recalling the advice that, 'You are your own master,' you can change what happens by taking action." Twitter, December 26, 2017, 7:30 p.m., https://x.com/DalaiLama/status/945602611251634181.

———. "The Purpose of Life Is to Be Happy." Originally published by *India Today*, September 30, 2021, available at DalaiLama.com, www.dalailama.com/messages/transcripts-and-interviews/the-purpose-of-life-is-to-be-happy.

David-Néel, Alexandra. *Magic and Mystery in Tibet.* Dover Publications, 1971.

Davidson, Richard J. "How Mindfulness Changes the Emotional Life of Our Brains." Video, 17 min., 52 sec. TEDxSanFrancisco, October 2019, www.ted.com/talks/richard_j_davidson_how_mindfulness_changes_the_emotional_life_of_our_brains_jan_2019/transcript?language=en.

Davis, Matthew, and Michael Farrell Scott. *Opening the Mountain: Circumambulating Mount Tamalpais, A Ritual Walk.* Counterpoint Press, 2006.

De Botton, Alain. *How Proust Can Change Your Life.* Pantheon, 1997.

## SOURCES AND WORKS CONSULTED

*The Dhammapada: Teachings of the Buddha.* Translated by Gil Fronsdal. Shambhala Publications, 2008.

*The Diamond Sutra and The Sutra of Hui-neng.* Translated by A. F. Price and Wong Mou-Lam. Shambhala Classics, 2005.

Didion, Joan. *The Year of Magical Thinking.* Knopf, 2005.

Duncan, David James. "The Mickey Mantle Koan." In *River Teeth: Stories and Writings*, 119–135. Random House, 2012.

———. "On Searching for Meaning and Solving a Koan of Loss." Interview by author. "Between-States: Conversations About Bardo and Life." *Tricycle: The Buddhist Review*, October 24, 2023, https://tricycle.org/article/david-james-duncan.

Duras, Marguerite. *Writing.* Translated by Mark Polizzotti. Brookline Books, 1998.

Febos, Melissa. *Girlhood.* Bloomsbury, 2021.

———. "Turning Toward a More Authentic Life." Interview by author. "Between-States: Conversations About Bardo and Life." *Tricycle: The Buddhist Review*, April 10, 2023, https://tricycle.org/article/melissa-febos.

Ferrante, Elena. "We Don't Have to Fear Change, What Is Other Shouldn't Frighten Us." Interview in *The Guardian*, August 29, 2020, https://www.theguardian.com/books/2020/aug/29/elena-ferrante-we-dont-have-to-fear-change-what-is-other-shouldnt-frighten-us.

Fields, Rick, and Benjamin Bogin. *How the Swans Came to the Lake: A Narrative History of Buddhism in America.* Shambhala, 2022.

Flaubert, Gustave. *The Selected Letters of Gustave Flaubert.* Translated by Francis Steegmuller. Farrar, Straus and Giroux, 1971.

Gardner, John. *The Art of Fiction.* Knopf, 1984.

Gilsinan, Kathy. "The Buddhist and the Neuroscientist: What Compassion Does to the Brain." *The Atlantic*, July 4, 2015, www.theatlantic.com/health/archive/2015/07/dalai-lama-neuroscience-compassion/397706.

Greer, Andrew Sean. "Creating a Sense of Joy." Interview by author. "Between-States: Conversations About Bardo and Life." *Tricycle:*

## SOURCES AND WORKS CONSULTED

*The Buddhist Review*, July 24, 2023, https://tricycle.org/article/andrew-sean-greer-joy.

Guy, David. "The Hermit Who Owned His Mountain: A Profile of W. Y. Evans Wentz." *Tricycle: The Buddhist Review*, Spring 1997, https://tricycle.org/magazine/hermit-who-owned-his-mountain.

Hamid, Mohsin. "Every Ending Is a Beginning." Interview by author. "Between-States: Conversations About Bardo and Life." *Tricycle: The Buddhist Review*, November 10, 2022, https://tricycle.org/article/mohsin-hamid-interview.

———. *The Last White Man: A Novel*. Penguin, 2023.

Hawthorne, Nathaniel. *The Scarlet Letter: A Romance*. Vintage Classics. Vintage, 2014.

Hayashi, Yukari, and Barrie McLean, dirs. *The Tibetan Book of the Dead: A Way of Life*. Alive Mind Media, 2008 [1994]. DVD. Quotations edited for readability.

Herrera, Hayden. *Frida: A Biography of Frida Kahlo*. Harper and Row, 1983.

Herrick, Mark. "Taking a Modern Look at the Burning House." *Tricycle: The Buddhist Review*, September 25, 2023, https://tricycle.org/article/lotus-sutra-burning-house.

Hilton, James. *Lost Horizon*. Simon and Schuster, 1960.

Horowitz, Alexandra. *On Looking: A Walker's Guide to the Art of Observation*. Simon and Schuster, 2013.

Jen, Gish. "Finding Your Own Narrative." Interview by author. "Between-States: Conversations About Bardo and Life." *Tricycle: The Buddhist Review*, March 7, 2023, https://tricycle.org/article/gish-jen.

Kafka, Franz. *The Metamorphosis*. Vanguard, 1946.

Karunatilaka, Shehan. *The Seven Moons of Maali Almeida*. Sort of Books, 2022.

Kawabata, Yasunari. *Snow Country*. Translated by Edward G Seidensticker. Pedigee Books, 1957, 1981.

Kay, Jeremy. "Alejandro G. Iñárritu on Finding the 'Higher Truth' in 'Bardo' and Why Biographies Are 'Lies and Hypocrisy.'" *Screen Daily*, November 30, 2022, www.screendaily.com/features/alejandro

-g-inarritu-on-finding-the-higher-truth-in-bardo-and-why-bio
graphies-are-lies-and-hypocrisy/5176955.article?adredir=1.
"Kengo Kuma. Sensing Spaces: Architecture Reimagined." Video, 5 min., 39 sec. YouTube, posted by Royal Academy of Arts, January 22, 2014, www.youtube.com/watch?v=Ew4rx6oQOgY. Quotation edited for readability.
Kenyon, Jane. "Otherwise." Poets.org, Academy of American Poets, https://poets.org/poem/otherwise.
Khamo. "About The Tibetan Book of the Dead." Liner notes for Laurie Anderson, Tenzin Choegyal, and Jesse Paris Smith, *Songs from the Bardo*, 2019, available at Smithsonian Folkways Recordings, https://folkways-media.si.edu/docs/folkways/artwork/SFW40583.pdf.
Killingsworth, Matthew A., and Daniel T. Gilbert. "A Wandering Mind Is an Unhappy Mind." *Science*, November 12, 2010, www.science.org/doi/10.1126/science.1192439?url_ver=Z39.88-2003&rfr_id=ori:rid:crossref.org&rfr_dat=cr_pub%20%200pubmed.
Lahiri, Jhumpa. *Unaccustomed Earth*. A. A. Knopf, 2008.
Leary, Timothy, Ralph Metzner, and Richard Alpert. *The Psychedelic Experience: A Manual Based on the Tibetan Book of the Dead*. New American Library, 1964.
*The Life of Milarepa*. Translated by Lobsang P. Lhalungpa. Penguin / Far West Translations, 1979.
Lopez, Donald. *The Tibetan Book of the Dead: A Biography*. Princeton University Press, 2011.
McPhee, John. *Annals of the Former World*. Farrar, Straus and Giroux, 1998.
———. "On Going into the Zone." Interview by author. "Between-States: Conversations About Bardo and Life." *Tricycle: The Buddhist Review*, December 6, 2022, https://tricycle.org/article/john-mcphee.
Metcalf, Franz. *What Would Buddha Do? 101 Answers to Life's Daily Dilemmas*. Simon and Schuster, 2002.
Montaigne, Michel de. *The Complete Essays*. Translated by M. A. Screech. Penguin, 2003.
Moore, Lorrie. *I Am Homeless If This Is Not My Home*. Knopf, 2023.

## SOURCES AND WORKS CONSULTED

Pakhoutova, Elena. "*Westworld* and Hidden Treasures." *Spiral*, March 21, 2018, https://rubinmuseum.org/westworld-and-hidden-treasures.

Pieiller, Evelyne. "Les révolutions de Rousseau." *Le Monde diplomatique*, October 2012, p. 27, www.monde-diplomatique.fr/2012/10/PIEILLER/48272.

Popova, Maria. *Figuring*. Vintage, 2020.

Proust, Marcel. *In Search of Lost Time*. Vol. 1, *Swann's Way*. Translated by Lydia Davis. Penguin 2002.

Rhodes, Nicholas, and Deki Rhodes. *A Man of the Frontier*. Mira Bose, 2006.

Ricard, Matthieu. *Happiness*. Atlantic Books, 2012.

Robertson, David. "The Circumambulation of Mt. Tamalpais." *Western American Literature* 30, no. 1 (1995): 3–28.

Saunders, George. *Lincoln in the Bardo*. Penguin Random House, 2017.

Schneider, David. *Crowded by Beauty: The Life and Zen of Poet Philip Whalen*. University of California Press, 2015.

"Scientist Inspired by Dalai Lama Studies Happiness." DalaiLama.com, May 15, 2010, www.dalailama.com/news/2010/scientist-inspired-by-dalai-lama-studies-happiness.

"73 Questions with Taylor Swift." Interview by Joe Sabia. Video, 9 min., 41 sec. YouTube, posted by Vogue, April 19, 2016, www.youtube.com/watch?v=XnbCSboujF4.

Shapiro, Dani. "This Moment Is the Only Moment." Interview by author. "Between-States: Conversations About Bardo and Life." *Tricycle: The Buddhist Review*, June 23, 2023, https://tricycle.org/article/dani-shapiro.

Shōnagon, Sei. *The Pillow Book of Sei Shōnagon*. Translated and edited by Ivan Morris. Penguin, 1971.

Slater, Ann Tashi. "Calcutta Evening." In *The Penguin Book of Modern Tibetan Essays*. Edited by Tenzin Dickie. Penguin, 2023.

———. "Circling the Mountain." *Kyoto Journal*, November 2013.

———. Darjeeling Journal (column). *Catapult*, 2019–2020, https://magazine.catapult.co/tag/darjeeling-journal.

## SOURCES AND WORKS CONSULTED

———. "Family Connection in a Teapot." *New York Times*, June 23, 2020, www.nytimes.com/2020/06/23/well/family/family-connection-in-a-teapot.html.

———. *HuffPost Blog*. 2012–2017, www.huffpost.com/author/atslater-642.

———. "In the Cave." *Kyoto Journal*, Summer 2021.

———. "A Journey Between Lives." *Tricycle: The Buddhist Review*, Summer 2021, https://tricycle.org/magazine/ann-tashi-slater-ancestors.

———. "Leaving the Palace." In *Wanting: Women Writing About Desire*. Edited by Margot Kahn and Kelly McMasters. Catapult, 2023.

———. "Lessons from My College Son, While We Were Home Together." *Washington Post*, April 30, 2021, www.washingtonpost.com/lifestyle/2021/04/30/lessons-from-college-son.

———. "Light and Shadow." *Narrative*, November 22, 2023. https://www.narrativemagazine.com/issues/stories-week-2022-2023/story-week/light-and-shadow-ann-tashi-slater.

———. "My Father, Montaigne, and the Art of Living." *Catapult*, October 29, 2020, https://magazine.catapult.co/culture/stories/ann-tashi-slater-books-essays-writing-my-father-and-michel-de-montaigne.

———. "Teatime in Darjeeling." *Tin House*, Winter 2017, https://tinhouse.com/teatime-in-darjeeling.

———. "Tibetan Butter Tea and Pink Gin." *Kyoto Journal*, September 2015, http://kyotojournal.org/asian-encounters/tibetan-butter-tea-and-pink-gin-life-in-old-darjeeling.

———. Tokyo Journal (column). *Catapult*, 2019, https://magazine.catapult.co/tag/tokyo-journal.

———. "Travelers." *Gulf Coast*, Winter/Spring 2012.

———. "Writing and *The Tibetan Book of the Dead*." *AGNI* (blog), August 13, 2018, https://agnionline.bu.edu/blog/writing-and-the-tibetan-book-of-the-dead.

Sogyal Rinpoche. *The Tibetan Book of Living and Dying*. Harper San Francisco, 1993.

## SOURCES AND WORKS CONSULTED

Stagg, Christopher. "The Hundred Thousand Songs of Milarepa: A New Translation." *Lion's Roar*, 2018, www.lionsroar.com/the-hundred-thousand-songs-of-milarepa-a-new-translation.

Takahashi, Munemasa. *Tsunami, Photographs, and Then*. Translated by Futoshi Miyagi. AKAAKA Art Publishing, 2014.

*The Tale of the Heike*. Translated by Helen Craig McCullough. Stanford University Press, 1988.

Talon, Emmanuelle. "L'arabe, une <<langue de France>> sacrifiée." *Le Monde diplomatique*, October 2012, p. 3, https://www.monde-diplomatique.fr/2012/10/TALON/48275.

Tan, Amy. *The Joy Luck Club*. G. P. Putnam's Sons, 1989.

Tanizaki, Jun'ichirō. *In Praise of Shadows*. Translated by Thomas J. Harper and Edward G. Seidensticker. Leete's Island Books, 1977.

*The Threefold Lotus Sutra: A Modern Translation for Contemporary Readers*. Translated by Michio Shinozaki, Brook A. Ziporyn, and David C. Earhart. Kosei Publishing, 2019.

*The Tibetan Book of the Dead*. Translated by Robert A. F. Thurman. HarperCollins, 1994.

*The Tibetan Book of the Dead: First Complete Translation*. Edited by Graham Coleman, with Thupten Jinpa. Translated by Gyurme Dorje. Penguin Books, 2005.

*The Tibetan Book of the Dead*, 2nd ed. Edited by W. Y. Evans-Wentz. Translated by Lāma Kazi Dawa-Samdup. Oxford University Press, 1949.

*The Tibetan Book of the Dead*, 3rd ed. Edited by W. Y. Evans-Wentz. Translated by Lāma Kazi Dawa-Samdup. Oxford University Press, 1960.

*The Tibetan Book of the Great Liberation*. Edited by W. Y. Evans-Wentz. Oxford University Press, 1954. Brackets in the original have been omitted.

Weil, Simone. *Gravity and Grace*. Translated by Arthur Wills. G. P. Putnam's Sons, 1952.

Winkler, Ken. *Pilgrim of the Clear Light: The Biography of Dr. Walter Evans-Wentz*, 3rd ed. Independently published, 2022. Kindle edition.

Witting, Amy. *A Change in the Lighting*. Viking Australia, 1994.

# RAISING READERS
## Books Build Bright Futures

Thank you for reading this book and for being a reader of books in general. As an author, I am so grateful to share being part of a community of readers with you, and I hope you will join me in passing our love of books on to the next generation of readers.

**Did you know that reading for enjoyment is the single biggest predictor of a child's future happiness and success?**

More than family circumstances, parents' educational background, or income, reading impacts a child's future academic performance, emotional well-being, communication skills, economic security, ambition, and happiness.

Studies show that kids reading for enjoyment in the US is in rapid decline:

- In 2012, 53% of 9-year-olds read almost every day. Just 10 years later, in 2022, the number had fallen to 39%.
- In 2012, 27% of 13-year-olds read for fun daily. By 2023, that number was just 14%.

Together, we can commit to **Raising Readers** and change this trend. How?

- Read to children in your life daily.
- Model reading as a fun activity.
- Reduce screen time.
- Start a family, school, or community book club.
- Visit bookstores and libraries regularly.
- Listen to audiobooks.
- Read the book before you see the movie.
- Encourage your child to read aloud to a pet or stuffed animal.
- Give books as gifts.
- Donate books to families and communities in need.

**Books build bright futures**, and **Raising Readers** is our shared responsibility.

For more information, visit **JoinRaisingReaders.com**

Sources: National Endowment for the Arts, National Assessment of Educational Progress, WorldBookDay.org, Nielsen BookData's 2023 "Understanding the Children's Book Consumer"